D1586537

THE BEST OF
ABOUT WOMEN

MARY CUMMINS

First published in 1996 by
Marino Books
16 Hume Street Dublin 2

Trade enquiries to CMD Distribution
55A Spruce Ave Stillorgan Industrial Park
Blackrock County Dublin

© Mary Cummins 1996

ISBN 1 86023 047 4

10 9 8 7 6 5 4 3 2 1

A CIP record for this title is available
from the British Library

Cover photo by Pat Whelan
courtesy of *The Irish Times*
Cover design: Bluett
Printed in Ireland by ColourBooks,
Baldoyle Industrial Estate, Dublin 13

CONTENTS

For My Mother

INTRODUCTION

In the environmentally correct language of the day, the About Women column is a truly organic creation. It has its roots in *The Irish Times* of the 1970s and 1980s – when women journalists campaigned ardently for the feminist cause in the old Women First and Our Times pages – and came into flower again naturally in the 1990s as an idea for a weekly comment piece, topical and wide-ranging, written by the Women's Affairs Correspondent. Backed by the Editor, Conor Brady, I launched into full broadside in September 1993 but neither he nor I could have anticipated the response, a steady river of letters from all parts of Ireland, week in and out.

And this is the rich source that has nourished About Women. Most of the letters are from women: personal accounts of how they live today, with hope, joy, anger and too often, pain and great sorrow. But men write too, in increasing numbers and with increasing thoughtfulness and concern about the present and future. At a very early point, I came to think of my work as the public part of an unseen network, one voice in a debate that is sometimes searching and slow, sometimes sharp and furious. It is to these hidden correspondents, the readers who write, that this book is dedicated with gratitude for all you have taught me. Long may your pens be at hand.

Publisher's note: a number of the pieces reproduced in this collection predate the formal establishment of the About Women column.

Prisoners of Fear

The murder of Patricia O'Toole (some of the details are given below) was one of the watershed cases that made women realise the bunkers of fear we now have to live in.

About three years ago, when travelling around the country, I often offered lifts to hitch-hikers. Male or female, it did not matter. Because I have hitched in the past I can empathise with their misery. But not any more. Now I don't even feel guilty if there is a lone figure standing in the rain on the bleak Dublin road outside Limerick or the stretch outside Portlaoise.

This change in my attitude has come about because of the huge increase in coverage of cases of violent crimes against women. Apart from the big, tragic or particularly horrific ones, there are cases reported where a woman was beaten up – perhaps sexually assaulted as well – even during a petty burglary in her own home. There is not a woman in the state who is not aware of the changed times. There is not a woman who is not aware that extreme youth or age will not save her from such violence. Your daughter is as vulnerable as your mother and as you are yourself. There is not a woman who is not aware that being crippled or pregnant will not avert a vicious attack. It happens every day.

Time was when we read about such crimes in the United States, in huge cities such as New York, and congratulated ourselves on living in a society where, by contrast, the key could be left in the door and people sleep easy in their beds – often with thousands of pounds stitched into the mattress. This change has affected everybody, but women were the first group to recognise it. They were the first to set about doing something. As well as establishing crisis centres and raising public awareness they held rallies and meetings to highlight the problems. Until recently many of their activities had taken place without much notice, praise or financial help. Things have changed a bit, but not enough.

Women are angry, seethingly angry, at the range of violent crimes against them that have become more and more commonplace. They are angry at the limits put on their activities because of these crimes. They are angry at the general acceptance that it is unsafe to drive in certain places at certain times of the day. And that anger is steadily increasing since the number of places and the times of day that are unsafe are growing. They have stretched into daylight hours and into areas close to public places. But alongside that anger, there is a feeling of helplessness. Women have become so accustomed to the danger of assault, rape or murder in an exceptionally short space of time that it was not unusual in recent weeks to hear women themselves use the circumstances of Patricia O'Toole's murder as an excuse for why the crime was committed.

Was she not foolish to have been out late on her own, foolish not to have accepted the offer of a friend to drive her home, foolish to have got lost in an area she did not know? Was she not outrageously foolish to have accepted help from a total stranger? For me, it is more frightening still to hear women accept these sorry arguments put forward by some men and to compound their effects by repeating them. It is inexcusable that they do not put pressure on every TD they vote for to change laws and attitudes which will help women to come forward and report a case, knowing they will not be victimised by the legal process. It is only since women have made strides in a variety of jobs that it has become clear that the way our world has been constructed contributes to making such crimes easier. It has taken women to point out the dangers inherent in the way housing estates have been built. They were designed for men in cars. They were designed to stop women taking an easy, casual stroll at any hour in roads where they will be visible and within shouting distance of neighbours.

For too long women have put up with the ever-increasing restrictions on their movements. They have put up with living under curfews, afraid of the night, afraid of going to the pictures in town, afraid of jogging in the local park early in the morning, afraid of offering lifts to hitch-hikers. Like others of their sex who are battered and abused in their own homes, they have gone along with the attitudes that have sent mothers rushing into refuges, their lives in chaos, leaving the men *in situ*.

The murder of Patricia O'Toole seems to have raised a particularly high level of concern and worry. This time there is more of a feeling that the circumstances causing that concern and worry must be dealt with, urgently. So what should be done? To start, I would hope that the subject

13

will be addressed at every level of authority and importance. For example, I would like to hear sermons and homilies in every church tomorrow on the subject. I want to hear politicians talking about what they are going to do. I want to hear clear commitments. I want them to consult women about what should be done. I want a national debate on the way our lives are going. Instead of more ads about securing houses, cars and valuables, I want to hear more people with influence telling me how we can live, work, walk and sleep. I do not want to go on waking to more horrendous stories. I want a climate where phrases like 'She asked for it' will be considered so awful that they will fade fast from the vocabulary.

23 January 1993

JOBS FOR THE GIRLS

I'll Just See If He's In, the title of the excellent 1996 BBC2 programmes on secretaries, aptly summarised the devalued/underestimated jobs that secretaries do. Most could do or are doing their bosses' jobs. Why do they persist with the charade? Maybe they should form a secretaries' support group and sack their bosses.

Yesterday, eleven women lost their jobs as Dáil secretaries in Leinster House. Only an eleventh-hour intervention by Fianna Fáil and SIPTU officials reduced the toll from twenty-three. Despite the fact that they had experience of between two and ten years, they were turned down, without discussion, by some new TDs, including Labour Party TDs–the main group with the ability to offer jobs.

A SIPTU official has confirmed that some of the new Labour TDs who refused to take the secretaries, who are now facing the dole queues, were women. These women TDs were high in the hope-stakes of the women of Ireland. They were the ones who knew, who understood, who were not going to take it any more. They would be to Ireland what Hillary Rodham Clinton was expected to be to the United States. We would all get a dole-out in the Clintonesque Camelot. Is the Irish dole-out just the dole?

The large number of Dáil secretaries out of a job results from the election in which Fianna Fáil and Fine Gael and, to a lesser extent, Democratic Left lost so many seats.

Labour and the Progressive Democrats are the only parties who increased their seats.

Many of the secretaries facing the appalling vista of adding their names to the State's 300,000 unemployed are women with children, mortgages and other commitments; several are single breadwinners. Dáil secretaries are among the lowest paid workers in the white-collar sector. Their salaries range from £146.90 a week to £312.46 a week – on a fifteen-point scale. To put it in perspective, a Fianna Fáil secretary I spoke to last week gets about £170 a week, after twelve years' experience. She has three children, one at third level. Ironically, last Friday the Dáil chamber spent a full day debating the recently published report of the second Commission on the Status of Women. Throughout the day, the parlous state of women's lives in Ireland today was exposed by a raft of speakers. There were nine men, including the Minister for Equality and Law Reform, Mervyn Taylor, and thirteen women. Six of them were new TDs. They included Joan Burton, Roisin Shortall and Eithne FitzGerald from Labour and Liz McManus from Democratic Left. They all made well crafted speeches, taking in almost every area of women's lives from birth to death. They were deadly serious and desperately depressing.

After the debate, I spoke to four Dáil secretaries. Our chat had been arranged in advance but as they spoke, what had been said for over five hours in the chamber rang hollow indeed. They were four angry women between the ages of twenty-five and thirty-six. The threat of twenty-three of their colleagues being let go had sparked off a fine rage that is simmering most of the time among the

16

women who work at this level in Leinster House. They know that they are some of the best, most intelligent, most committed women workers around. Not only do they have to know the law, they have to be able to deal with constituents on the telephone. They may have to pretend that the TD is in the chamber or at a meeting or busy. They do most of the work of 'getting' things for constituents. They are continually dealing with other government departments, health boards, priests, doctors, teachers and schools, banks and counsellors.

They have to be discreet with their own colleagues and also about their bosses. They complain of 'attitude harassment' – the 'you're just the girl in the office' line. They say they feel the vibes of 'you're not one of us' if they get into the lift with a TD of some seniority. This, they stress, comes both from women and men. They even have a 'lift list' which is totally confidential between themselves, and they pass on the names to newcomers. It names the men you never, but never, get into the lift with on your own. It is updated regularly.

The secretaries usually do not use the Dáil self-service restaurant where you can get snacks or a good meal for what is generally regarded as a good price. These women do not earn enough to afford 'a good price'. Many bring in their own sandwiches. But there is no rest room. 'So if your man is in the office, you can't take them out and eat them. You can end up eating them in the ladies,' said one with a shrug.

At least six hours' overtime a week is mandatory if life is to be worth living. At election time, they head for the

17

constituency, no matter where it is in the country – 'and you buy your own train ticket' – and for the duration of the campaign some run the candidate's house, mind the kids, answer the phone. Do everything and anything. With no extra pay. The odd drink. What comes through very strongly is the frustration at being so invisible – not just within their offices but in Leinster House and in the wider world.

'At the most he (the TD) will say, "we did a good job there",' said another. The constituents assume they are just the nice girls who cajole their bosses into getting things done for them. And then, at the end of the day, if the boss loses his seat, they are dumped. Maybe the twenty-three who are now out in the cold should form a Group 23? What takers?

2 March 1993

NORMAL NORMA

Another courageous woman who refused to conform.

Some women can do no right. Across the Atlantic Hillary Clinton is annoying people to death because hardly had her husband won the presidency when she affirmed all the dire forebodings and forecasts of what she would and would not do, once inside the White House. She smartly put her maiden name, Rodham, back where she had always wanted it and moved into power.

In direct contrast, across the Irish Sea, Norma Major is continuing to make people apoplectic simply because she refuses to get desperately involved in her husband's job. She has been abused, slighted, laughed at and even allocated a special psychological jargon term to describe her perceived failure to perform for the cameras and the columnists. She loves her own home, behaves like a lioness in protecting her children from the media and runs her husband's constituency with dedicated devotion. But is that enough? No way.

The same kind of negative focus is applied here to women who make it up the ladder, particularly in politics. Remember the recent *Late Late Show* when some of the new women TDs were all asked – as if they were naughty teenagers caught breaking curfew – who was at home minding their children? The fact that each one of them was at least thirty-something and already had a full-time job and a father for her children apparently did not count. The implication was that they were wanton in some way because they had got a job, a job usually held by a man. No matter what they do, they can't win. That is if they take any notice of those who insist on infringing their rights of privacy. Many of them, unfortunately, are women journalists who pursue these women as if, because they are women themselves, they have some God-given right to harry their quarries with savage intensity.

Some excuse could possibly be made for looking closely at new women TDs. Because of their increased numbers and the breakthrough this represents in Irish attitudes, a case could be made for studying them in more depth. Also, because Hillary Rodham Clinton is unlike any previous First Lady – she has ditched the term as well as the role that went with it – she is worthy of study. But Norma Major is a totally different case.

Acres of newsprint have been dedicated to this woman who married a Lambeth Tory councillor who went on to take the highest office in British political life. While John Major went onwards and upwards, Norma has been lampooned for obviously having a talent that most people – men and women – would kill for. She is single-minded and refuses to be used as a prop for her husband's photocalls. Her sin, according to the British media, is that she simply won't play the game according to the dated old rules. In fact, in many ways, she and Hillary Rodham have much in common. Both turned things around to suit themselves.

A private and reserved woman, Norma Major has followed her husband's leaps in her own paced way. She has stubbornly refused to become part of the circus unless it suits her. She is happiest in her home at Huntingdon and uses Number 10 only when she has to. She has got to like Chequers and by demystifying it has drawn more ire and catty comments from commentators. Having previously spurned the privileged town apartments and country estates that went with the various jobs her husband held in the Cabinet, she began to use Chequers like any ordinary weekend retreat and is about to write a book about it. She invites old friends and new and the whole thing is stunningly informal but the British establishment, which seem to be suffering from great post-colonisation stress, find all this very difficult to accept. They concentrate on her clothes, which never seem to them to be quite the thing. Most of the British newspapers have called in analysts, from way-out types to 'distinguished experts', to tell them what to make of this perfectly nice, sensible, loyal and kind woman – and that is what you read at the end of it all. They came up with a variety of diagnoses, each more daft than the last.

To the outsider, what seems to be at the core of the bitterness and criticism dumped on Norma Major is her own and her husband's working-class background. But while her husband is almost always analysed in the context of the job he is doing and how his background is a positive plus in a Britain plummeting swiftly to the bottom, all her perceived sins are related to the fact that Lambeth is not the place to prepare you to be a top spouse.

The vicious attacks on Norma Major are an obvious extension of criticism of women who manage to make it into the public arena – albeit by extension. In a new, unauthorised biography to be published shortly by Fourth Estate, the author, Tim Walker, catalogues Ms Major's life and times in intense and thorough detail. He admits that while his subject did not want to be involved she gave carte blanche to her closest and very loyal friends to talk to him freely. To me this does not suggest an insecure, anxiety-ridden woman, 'like a rabbit caught in headlamps' as one reporter described her.

What it seems to show is a woman not interested in politics and who is showing a terrific and healthy resistance to all the reams of wounding criticism that have been showered on her. Tim Walker's book, entitled *Norma*, is a good but infinitely depressing read. All through it, one is conscious of the absence of any first-hand information from the woman herself. What I want to hear is the woman's own story instead of yet more selected quotes, comparisons with Glenys Kinnock and Judy Ashdown and previous spouses of Number 10. Go for it, Norma. Knock them dead.

23 March 1993

WILL THEY BE REWARDED IN HEAVEN?

I get up early and am usually in the office before 7 am so I have got to know some of the 'faceless' women who clean up after the ravages of the previous day. They are the unsung and dismally rewarded heroes who do the most basic but desperately necessary work. Our hypocrisy towards them is evident in the poll mentioned here.

Earlier this year an MRBI [Market Research Bureau of Ireland] poll showed that women working as office cleaners came second (at 55 per cent) in the ratings of the esteem in which women are regarded by other women. Full-time wives and mothers came first at 75 per cent. Sportswomen rated 40 per cent, followed by: nuns (36 per cent); paid working mothers (40 per cent); women politicians (33 per cent) and women journalists at the bottom, rating 27 per cent.

Who are office cleaners? They are now mostly employed by large contract cleaning firms, which has added to the anonymity surrounding their work. They come and go at unsocial hours, mostly when large office blocks are empty, early in the morning and late at night. They are the good fairies who get the desk you left in chaos back to a tidy, shining and manageable work space.

Who are they? What are they paid? What lives do they lead when they are not tidying yours up?

Mary is in her mid-thirties. She lives in one of the large sprawling estates in Blanchardstown in west Dublin. For most of the year, she goes to work in the dark and goes home in the dark. Her husband is unemployed and they have four dependent children. She has been working the unsocial hours demanded for the job for most of her married life because it allows her to work as well as being available for her family.

'The alarm goes off at ten to five. I'm up about five, struggling. I hit the bathroom and then the kitchen to make a cup of tea. I just keep moving. It's a bit of a walk to the bus. I'm there by twenty to six and it's another day. I work from six until half past eight. Getting up is terrible, especially in the winter. It's cold, freezing cold. It could be lashing rain. It could be snowing. It's so dark. You could forget it in this weather when it's bright but the thought of the winter is always there at the back of your mind. I often say if I won the Lotto I'd stay in bed in the mornings just for spite. You have to be well organised but sometimes I could be ironing a uniform at ten past five on a Monday morning. My husband gets them up and out to school but I leave everything ready. It's my own personal bit of pride. I like to think they'll go out to school clean and tidy. My girls are older but when they were younger you'd be rushing to get home, to make sure they have their hair right. I leave the breakfast table set the night before. I make the lunches. The uniforms are ready. The schoolbags are sitting near the door.'

It is 9 am and Mary has finished her two-and-a-half-hour shift as a cleaning woman in a big block of offices in the centre of Dublin. She is employed by a firm of contract cleaners with whom she has little contact. For her work, she is paid £3.50 an hour plus 60 pence a day towards her bus fare. It comes to just under £55 a week. This is the maximum she can earn without her husband, who is unemployed, losing some of the £145 a week he gets from social welfare for himself, Mary and their four children, aged from seven to seventeen.

She works every day from Monday to Friday and on Saturdays every second week. They live 'in fear, always the fear' that for some unknown bureaucratic reason, her husband's welfare money will be cut. It has not happened but you can never tell, she says, what 'they' will get up to. For her husband to take any job that he has been offered in recent years would mean an instant drop in earnings for the family, she says. She shrugs at the idiocy of it.

Mary works alone on a large, open-plan floor and often works the whole shift without speaking to another person. 'The first thing I do is switch on the radio. I don't even listen to it but it's there in the background. I kind of lose myself in what I'm doing.' Mary has a round, cherubic face and a mop of curly dark hair. She is good-humoured and devastatingly philosophical. 'You'd have to be. If it was affecting my life at home, I'd jack it in.'

She gets paid every two weeks. 'With £100 you can do something. You can pay a bill and maybe buy one of the children a pair of shoes or something. We don't go out, except maybe on Tuesdays when I get paid and if it's a week when the children's allowance is due. Just out to the pub for a couple of drinks. We might go out for something

25

special on our anniversary. Last year we went away for a weekend. It was great, but for holidays it's the Costa del Dollymount.' She gets two weeks' paid holidays and, she thinks, about four or five days in the winter. 'The worst part of the job is probably the toilets. They are fine in the company – and the men clean the men's toilets – but once when I worked in a factory on an industrial estate, I used to nearly get sick when I went in to clean the men's urinals.'

Even though most of the women travel long distances from satellite towns such as Tallaght and Clondalkin and beyond, they are not provided with a bus service. They would have to pay about £10 each a week if they took a private bus between them. Mary says most cannot afford that. She lives in Blanchardstown and has a brisk fifteen-minute walk to the bus. On the way she meets up with other women, most in the same jobs. She buys a weekly bus ticket for £10.50 but can use it at other times of the day. 'Your work has to be up to standard. If they have faults to find you'll hear about them. You get two written warnings and one verbal one and then you can be sacked,' she says.

She usually gets home by 10.30 am and rarely goes back to bed during the day. 'Sometimes, by Thursday, the sleep would catch up with you and you might go but once you're awake it's hard to go back.'

25 May 1993

NOT IRON,
MORE THE IRONIC LADY

Regardless of what others think of her policies Margaret Hilda fascinates me. She is one of the few women who will go raging into the next millennium.

For years I have felt like getting a special T-shirt with 'I luv Thatcher' scrawled across it. The only problem is it would have to be worn only in the privacy of one's own home. Even there it could cause trouble. For a card-carrying feminist, there are special difficulties. She is the thorn that gets in the way of great relationships with women with whom I agree on almost every other subject under the sun and moon.

They do not understand me and I cannot fathom the narrow-focused way they see her. What I have never understood is the series of emotions running from angst to frothing vituperation that Margaret Thatcher evokes. Even if some people admire her – apart from Ronald Reagan – they nearly always have to qualify their views. They say they like her . . . but. They don't agree with what she did to the miners, the way she speaks, the floppy bows on the blouses she wore for years, what she did to Britain. And so on. Now that she is back centre stage again with her memoirs of the Downing Street years, all the aggro that had receded a bit since she was heaved is out in the open. She is the subject of endless opinion, speculation and bitching.

After his interview with her last week, Gay Byrne told the nation that one woman had rung to say she was turning off her set until that woman was off. During the interview and following it, there were many more calls complaining about her, most of them from women. They all confirmed the fact that the lady is truly fascinating and the effect she has on people is ditto. Professor Anthony Clare's call to G. B. (he was one of the many who telephoned the show) was probably more riveting than the interview itself. For a consummate broadcasting professional who regularly gets the great, the good, the foolish and the famous to sit in front of him and bare their hearts and souls to the nation on BBC's Radio 4, Clare sounded as awestruck as a schoolboy. He was bewitched, bothered and intrigued. It sounded as if he could stay on all day, trying to find a place for this woman who obviously did not fit any of the shapes of the hundreds of women he has dealt with both as a psychiatrist and an investigator. Was it a case of she-who-will-not-be-defined?

I first saw Lady T. just over ten years ago in the course of the 1983 election campaign when she swept the grateful (if ungracious) Tories to a landslide victory. Before that I had read all the usual stuff, taken the Iron Lady imagery that abounded, the bossy-boots representation, the Boadicea effigies that surrounded her. I had read her triumphalist 'this lady's not for turning' speech. And much more. What converted me was seeing her up close for a full day on one of her whistle-stop campaign trips around the country.

That day it was the midlands and the first stop was

Stoneleigh Abbey, an agricultural college near Coventry. We were waiting in the drizzling rain outside the abbey. 'Rule Britannia' was booming from behind the stately walls. Up the long, winding drive she came, perched rather uneasily on a trailer drawn at funereal pace by a tractor. She was dressed in shades of blue and had a scarf draped around her head. It was the scarf that did it. It was the way she wore it that made the scales fall from my previously media-blinded eyes. She is a woman, I shrieked to myself. It was my first and abiding impression and has coloured my views of her ever since.

It was the way she sat primly on the trailer. But more so, it was the scarf. She was just like a woman who had been for the weekly set and did not want her hair disturbed for at least a few hours. The scarf sat on top of her hair, tied loosely under the chin. Her face also looked as if she had just come from under the drier. The forehead was a bit shiny, the powder gone a bit from the cheeks and the lipstick reduced to a lick. Immediately I could see other women of her age. I could see my mother. I could see myself. No matter what she had done in the Falklands, what she had done to the workers, what she would go on to do in the future, that image of a woman overshadowed or shaded every other impression I'd had of Lady T.

Later that day, I stayed close, gobsmacked by this new, shattering discovery. I watched her in dozens of situations until later that night she packed a hall of over five thousand and did her PM thing in the way I was used to seeing her. But it is the other images that have always lingered. I remember the way she walked quickly, with a little run, like older women do – from the knees down. She reminded me of women in supermarkets, plucking things off shelves because they know exactly where they are and running on quickly. Like them, she had no time to dawdle. She sweated freely as the crowds at an ideal homes exhibition surged around her; little rivulets running down her forehead. She looked over her shoulder frequently to see if Denis was at her shoulder. He always was.

Later in the day that image was all tarted up for the cameras, the autocue and the blazing speech to the troops and the pollsters. At press conferences in that campaign she was in her element, calling on the men in her most hectoring tones . . . 'Norman . . . Geoffrey . . . ' And they stood up and answered, meek as lambs. It was the first time I had seen a woman in a position to treat men with the same arrogance and patronage as men. Boy, it was good. There are more women at it now, but ten years ago, she shed the light. That woman made waves.

Since her resignation, she has been accused of worse things than when she was in office (if that is possible). What most people seem to find most exasperating is the fact that she will not go away. She will not retire to the dower house like a dutiful elder statesperson. She stays. She niggles. She terrifies the life out of the party for fear of what she will say or do next. And still they know they may yet need her.

I have no difficulty with her behaviour. She is behaving exactly like any rejected wife, since politics is her real spouse. Trailing Major or getting ahead of him, doing chat shows around the world as if she were still in charge and hanging on to the sleeve of power as fervently as she does – this is all what I would expect. Are jilted women not doing it all the time in every country?

Only she does it better. Hang in there, Lady T. You have closets of admirers waiting for your comeback.

26 October 1993

I BLAME THE MEDIA

*They come to Ireland at all times, these foreign writers
and journalists, but particularly when issues to do with
abortion, divorce or sex scandals are in the news. They
come with their minds made up and disappear again
after begging us to meet them for a few hours to explain
the Irish situation. When you read what they eventually
write you wonder if you dreamt the whole thing, since
what they have to say is such total fiction.*

There are two books out at present featuring Irish women.
Linda Grant's waddles from turgid to incomprehensible. It
is the sort of book you would never read unless you had a
special interest. I have.

Rosemary Mahoney's (pronounced Mahowney) is a load
of corny rubbish suitable for whatever section of the US
market believes that while we don't have real pigs in the
kitchen any more, the people in the kitchen are not much
better.

You might read Mahoney's *Whoredom in Kimmage: Irish
Women Coming of Age* and throw it away. But I met
Mahoney several times and both she and Grant have to be
put in the context of the hordes of journalists, writers,
you-name-its who shot into the country in 1991 and 1992,
looking for 'the real Ireland'. They come with a mindset
about Irish women. Irish women equal the X case, condoms,
abortions, the Kerry Babies, Granard and Mary Robinson

in that order. And they do not really want to know much about the President.

In 1991 and 1992, the X case, abortion and recollections of the Kerry Babies was what they were stuck with. Like terriers trying to get the last bit of gristle off a bone, they gave you a headache when you tried to explain time and again that not *all* Irish women spend their weekends having abortions or burying their babies. Not all Irish men go around with hurleys knocking women into back lanes and ravishing them. You could see their eyes glaze over when you told them that Irish women have acres more maternity leave than the paltry two weeks in the US. You could tell them about the Second Commission on the Status of Women and the Council for the Status of Women. Did they want to know? Did they what? You could tell them about the phenomenon of the mushrooming women's groups around the country doing everything from the Leaving Certs to setting up their own businesses. They fiddled, stifled yawns and went straight down the alphabet to X again.

Grant's book, *Sexing the Millennium*, is the more awful of the two. She has just one chapter on Ireland, entitled 'The Country Run by Men in Dresses'. It is not only factually inaccurate in several places (for instance according to her Dev was the first President, the Kerry babies episode happened in Caherciveen when it was Abbeydorney) but also confusing in its fast forward, fast backwards style, which leaves the reader totally unclear as to whether events happened last year or twenty years ago.

The penny was only beginning to drop when I had spent a tiring day covering a major women's conference. I found myself pinned against a wall in Jury's Hotel giving Grant all the details of the X case and realised she seemed not even to have read one report about it. She was ecstatic about the conference that day. Just imagine, she said, fumbling for words, not since the mid-1970s had she ever seen the likes of 300 or so women gathered together in one place discussing their lives with heat and passion.

But is there a word about that in the book? (This is her first book.) No way, José. It simply runs from Kerry Babies to Granard to abortions and condoms. The way she does it, the late 1960s contraceptives train might as well have been last Saturday.

She writes: 'Conservatives dream of a world in which the sexual revolution never took place. What could such a country look like? In Ireland, abortion, homosexuality and divorce are, at the time of writing (this year) illegal. Contraception can be obtained by married couples from a handful of family planning clinics that struggle with no state support. You can buy a packet in Dublin but not in the villages where the pharmacist, the doctor, the priest and the policeman all watch out vigilantly for the wellbeing of their neighbours' souls.'

And there is more and more of that mix-mismatch that would have the average Irish hamlet chortling at the crossroads.

Mahoney, meanwhile, is making a bundle in the US, hitting the chart-toppers with her spiel: 'While the Irish have a genius for scorn, most often they choose to express it in a glancingly witty and satirical fashion that precludes any real expression of anger, renders them inculpable and soothes their dread of confrontation. An outright personal attack is uncommon.'

When she is not shovelling dirt on the real people, Mahoney uses little parables like this, just old-hat descriptions of the Irish that are repeated *ad nauseam* in every language about us . . . But they lend a little authority to canny authors working on wings and prayers to put together a book. She also has a long whinge about time: 'Lateness was a particularly Irish characteristic. The Irish took their social appointments remarkably lightly. When they said they would meet at seven o'clock, what they really meant was 7.40 or better yet, eight o'clock, or really, any old time they got around to getting there . . . Living in Ireland surrounded by such seemingly casual unconcern, I began to wonder if my own hyperpunctuality wasn't a terrible psychic burden.'

Mahoney and her burdens should not be let loose. She speaks little except when she is asking a favour, like can she write the story of your life. She describes the people of Corofin with a detail that makes them all sound like the worst of the *Punch* cartoons, which showed the Irish as animals of one sort or another. She describes what she presumes are their illicit relationships, their alcoholism and plenty more. All the sort of bog-stuff that some Americans love to believe about what they still call the ould sod. She has reams on lesbians, on women with IRA-spawned babies, on the Legion of Mary and the like. It is so awful and so babblingly bad that you can only laugh bleakly at the end of the day. After you have smashed a few plates.

Like most of the quick-buck merchants who came and

saw and made up their own minds, Mahoney makes vast sweeping judgements and generalisations. I have made several attempts to find out from her publishers when the book will be published here and they are evasive. They are not sure.

Eavan Boland invited her to her home. Mahoney got a flipping good interview about writing, Ireland, women and men and much more. But the interview only comes after she has described Boland's home and children with the purple precision of a trained voyeur. Eavan Boland's house 'was the modern sort the Irish call American . . . furniture in the small sitting-room arranged in a haphazard fashion. A low coffee table so overloaded with trinkets and figurines, tiny carvings, painted eggs, a pocket watch and other small, highly detailed artefacts that the table's surface was barely visible . . . another coffee table equally crowded . . . the impression of a householder in the process of cleaning out her attic and not knowing where to put things for the moment . . . she handed me a wide-bottomed mug shaped like a nuclear reactor . . . neither of us had any place to rest our mugs . . . '

Absolute drivel. And did she have an undercover camera as well? It was when I read this and a similar piece about Ruth Riddick I realised there are times when you have to count your blessings.

I met Mahoney a few times and gave her a lot of information. I took many telephone calls from public call boxes. At one stage I got worried. Mahoney seemed to be on an endless shuttle on buses between Tallaght and Ballymun. She trotted out stories of women; bleeding, battered women. They all seemed to have children in double figures – mostly by different men. The men she described were usually manic beasts. Yes, yes I said. There probably are some like that. But not all. Since she was writing a book I thought she should get it right. I made a date to cook a vat of pasta, invite a few knowledgeable women in different fields so that she could get a picture of Ireland 1991. I owe you one, Guardian Angel, because I had to cancel it at the last minute. Work intervened. If it had not, I know that I would be minus three good friends and would be cursing myself for leaving my cuteness behind when I left Kerry. My cosy little shebeen would be described in tawdry detail.

Her relieved reaction was slightly puzzling at the time. She would go to Clare and be back, she said breezily. Only now I know she did not want anything about the real Ireland. Fiction, passing as faction, is always a better headline grabber.

When she had finally left after phoning the latest gruesome despatch, a book she had written about China arrived from her publishers. It is a pretty and polished production but my blood ran cold. It described a year she had spent on student-swap on the campus of a college in a remote but infinitely recognisable part of China, I imagine, for Chinese people. It was an intimate account of all the principal players she met – many of them disaffected and depressed. This was the year before Tiananmen Square, before all hell broke loose. Everybody was described in vivid detail. It was frightening when one realised the repercussions it could have for the people who obviously thought she was their friend. But it was also riddled with that sort of intrusion into people's lives that brings you out in bumps of embarrassment. The *Kimmage* book is exactly the same.

They came in droves in 1991 and 1992. Like a plague of latter-day Huns they tumbled out of planes, boats, buses and trains from all parts of the (mostly Western) world. They invaded the lives of anybody they could get copy from. They ate our food, drank our drinks, slithered their way into our confidence and homes with cute or flattering plámás. One day you thought the State-siders were the worst. Next day a new-age journalist from Wapping would swiftly change your mind. There was one who not only picked your brain but rewrote your stories. There were many others. Most, by comparison with Mahoney and Grant, were plaster saints.

There is an unwritten international rule that says that journalists help each other out, particularly when you are working outside your own patch. More often than not it works. Every journalist has terrific memories of arriving in a strange town, city, country with a case of file cuttings and a head bursting with facts and figures – often contradictory. Every journalist remembers the locals who took them aside and patiently separated the reality from the fantasy; who explained all the facts, the different factions. They saved your life and your job.

That rule is Not-OK any more. Not for women anyway. And definitely not for women writing about Irish women. No more leeches. No more locusts acting out being a reporter or writer. No siree.

16 November 1993

SHADY PINES –
ALL OUR FUTURES?

*I think I unintentionally upset more women with this piece
than any other – women weighed down with quiet helplessness because their mothers were in nursing homes.
However, I still believe that it is a feminist issue and it is
only women who will restore some semblance of sanity to
the idiotic lives we are all leading trying to do it all.*

'Don't ever put me in a home, will you?' my mother asked.
Her tone was half-jokey. We both knew it was no joke. The
plea was real. Under the lightness was a cry from the heart.
That was nearly two years ago.

We had just left a nursing home in Dublin where a
friend of hers was convalescing after a heart attack. Mrs
B., in her eighties, would not be there for long. She had
two daughters, one a saint, the other a solid support. She
was around to be relied on. But she was busy with a young
family. She and her husband worked full-time. Mrs B. knew
she would be going to the saintly daughter in a week or so.
Then she would go back down the country to her own home.

That nursing home was handily set in the inner suburbs.
Mrs B. was sharing a room with three others, each paying
nearly £200 a week. The room was as near as dammit to a
semi-private hospital ward with minuscule lockers, pull-
around blinds and beige walls. Linoleum covered the floors
from the door in. There were a few holy pictures, a few

statues. It was grand, Mrs B. said. The nurses were so nice and fine it made up for everything. And she would be gone in a week anyway. She worried away at her rosary beads as she cracked jokes. She was stoical as she had been all her life. An intensely political woman, she was thirsting for news about C. J. H. – it was the run up to his final days in politics. She was aching to dissect the Fianna Fáil Party, to argue with her usual authority about the state of the nation. We tried. But in whispers it was not the same. The woman in the next bed was lying on her side, listless. Or listening?

I wandered off to get some fresh water along a corridor interrupted by closed white doors. The sitting room was behind one of them. A television was blaring in a far corner. All the chairs that circled it were taken. One or two of the elderly men and women were looking at the flickering set. The others were silent. Some had dozed off, their mouths slack. Others were looking into the distance. Some had their heads bowed. I fled.

The nurse downstairs, who was getting the pills out of the medicine cabinet, chatted while we arranged the flowers. She was a sensible, middle-aged woman. She lived locally and worked nights. As they went, and for the price, the home was not at all bad, she said. She had worked in others . . . She hesitated. The food was good. Dr X was always on call. The relations were good at visiting . . . or some of them anyway. Wasn't Mrs B. lucky? she said cheerily. The subject was dropped.

Back upstairs the sitting room was being evacuated. It was coming up to 8 pm. A young aide was jollying her charges along, taking some of them by the arm. Every few paces she stopped to direct the traffic: 'Not there, Ellen, the next one. Tom, you know you're upstairs.' They were still fully dressed but all wore slippers. So they slopped rather than walked. Their silent, softly-shod feet crept warily along the shiny corridor. It was an instant image of any institution where the people (patients? clients? inmates? customers?) are controlled.

The two other women from Mrs B.'s room came in. We chatted briefly. They pulled their curtains round to prepare for bed. Mrs B.'s eyes filled with tears as we left. Yes, she had all she wanted in the *Irish Press.* We would come again soon. We promised.

Mrs B. did leave. She went home and died in peace some months later, surrounded by her family. That single visit was a mirror of several to a variety of nursing homes over recent years. Some are expensive with single rooms and sea views. Others are run-down but regarded as adequate.

While Mrs B. is at rest now, I am far from peaceful. I rail against the society which, in a hop and a skip of one generation, is consigning its oldies to reservations. Unreservedly, I condemn this sanctimonious country populated by people who bless themselves and push their mothers and fathers into institutions, sanitised with names straight out of Trollope, Beatrix Potter or picked from the litany of saints.

'But she/he is happy there,' they whine. 'She/he doesn't know us any more ... ' She/he really needs professional care' ... 'I mean, like, how could we do it. We're out at work. The children need us. You should see their homework. We have our own lives. I would be insane. I would crack up.

41

She/he is better with strangers. Sure, she/he is having a great time. Bridge and chat. They can come and go. Mammy's friend can even have her car there. Much better for all of us. You should have seen her/him before . . . becoming impossible . . . couldn't please them . . . the worry . . . God knows it's awful visiting her/him sometimes.'

They nag on in the special voices retained for denial, for blustering their way out of consciences laden with well-deserved guilt. But their guilt is not half as heavy as they deserve. It is leavened by their friends, colleagues and neighbours who console one another they are doing their best for the betterment of everyone. Their nagging doubts are further alleviated by the elders-who-are-not-yet-oldies. Is there a bishop, a minister, a priest, any figure of authority who has ever said this is not how things should be?

In her latest book, *The Fountain of Age*, one of the mothers of feminism, Berry Friedan, deals with old age. Coming from the United States, which dreamed up, nurtured and refined the internment of old people, her argument against institutional care rings a bit hollow. Particularly since she throws in her own lifestyle as if it could be the norm. About nursing homes and their ilk, she writes: 'Depression, unhappiness, rigidity and low energy, intellectual ineffectiveness, negative self-image, feelings of personal insignificance and impotency, low range of interests, withdrawal, unresponsiveness to others and a tendency to live in the past rather than the future all seem to go along with "a view of self as old" in such settings.'

Friedan is right. Her problem is that she is about half a century too late in using the issue to keep her name in the lights. What is really more than a bit off is her own life and the grand way she is living ' . . . moving back and forth between my apartment in the dirty, noisy city of New York, my little house in Sag Harbour where I write and my children bring their children and my sub-let condos in California where I teach in the winter . . . ' Friedan feels a 'sharper relish – a new need for truth-telling'. If she works hard enough at it, maybe she'll get a bit part in *The Golden Girls*.

What is vividly clear is that, apart from writing what everybody knows anyway, she is not setting a new agenda for feminists on the question of old age. It is not enough to wait until you are an oldie yourself to fight for oldie-quotas in the Dáil, the Seanad, all kinds of councils and authorities. Each of us knows that every oldie in the country has a separate and rich experience, wisdom, emotion and detachment which must be used – not abused. It is there to be fed into every area of life. The only group aware of that, and using it, is the travelling community where the extended family is still the norm. It works.

And forget about the men out there. Once again, they do not want to know. Until they have to. In the meantime, they, and every whinging daughter/niece/grand-daughter should be forced to look at videos, as they slurp the cornflakes. The videos should show the worst of what lies ahead of them – stuck to a commode, being urged to eat up their greens and worse – if they do not liven up and change the world.

No doubt there are many people contented and grateful to be in nursing homes. Some may have even admitted themselves. And of course there are families for which it is the only option. But I do not want to go out whispering in a Shady Pines. I do not want it for my mother.

23 November 1993

WHO'S AFRAID OF NAOMI WOLF?

Wolf and Susan Faludi are two of the best of the younger feminist analysts and writers. Wolf is continually pushing out the boundaries and upsetting the previous generations who carved out the commandments of the sixties and seventies.

Ten minutes into a conversation with Grace last week, I sent up a silent prayer for Naomi Wolf: for her onward and upwards progression in setting out new markers for women. Victim-feminism gone. Power-feminism in.

With Wolf around, you can think clearly. You can forget about the Katie Roiphes and Camille Paglias, who are determined to make waves and secure bank accounts by being as contrary as possible; by setting back the fragile progress of women as far as they can. Wolf would put Grace straight on how to come to grips with real life.

Last week, Grace (one of many middle-aged, middle-class women who have been ignominiously dumped by their husbands and who regularly ring anonymously from various parts of the country with their fears, their isolation, their inability to talk to the friends they had when they were part of a couple) brought me up to date on the new worries in her life. Having left over two years ago, her husband is now trying to get her to waive her rights to the family home, she said. Under the Succession Act she

45

believes she would have one-third of its value if he dies after making a will. The house is big but now she is finding it impossible to maintain. Her children range in age from twenties to teens. The picture she paints of her husband and their lives is pretty awful but not unusual. On the outside, they were an envied, successful couple running a thriving family business. On the inside, they had a rotten marriage. She put up with put-downs, verbal abuse, silence, humiliation in front of their children. She learnt to be quiet, to go to her room and sob silently.

Her life now is still totally defined by her husband who is living with a new woman. The bills he will pay. The bills he will not. Grace is obsessed with the minutiae of what his solicitor said to hers and *vice versa*. Recently, her eldest son unsuccessfully tried to get his father to fork out a bit more money. When he came off the phone, Grace said how she wished she had not spent years working in her husband's business without demanding cash payment. Why had she not developed a career and life of her own?

'Yes,' asked her exasperated son. 'Why didn't you?' Instead, she had accepted the trappings of the big comfortable house, the several holidays a year, the good clothes, her own car and all the rest.

Despite having made significant advances in the past year, Grace is still heavily into what Naomi Wolf describes in *Fire with Fire*, her latest book, as 'victim feminism'. Wolf's thesis, briefly, is that the days for sitting around and moaning while accepting that men continue to call the shots are over. For a variety of reasons women have to come to terms with power-feminism. *Fire with Fire* in no way demeans the feminist works that have preceded it, but it is the healthy, natural and welcome progression in the literature of the women's movement. Wolf writes: 'Victim-feminism casts women as sexually pure, mystically nurturing and stresses the evil done to these "good" women as a way to petition for rights. Power-feminism sees women as human beings – sexual, individual, no better or worse than their male counterparts – and lays claim to equality simply because women are entitled to it. Victim feminist assumptions about universal female goodness and powerlessness and male evil are unhelpful in the new moment for they exalt what I've termed "trousseau reflexes" – outdated attitudes which women need least right now.'

While she understands why it exists, Wolf says: 'Victim feminism is obsolete because female psychology and the conditions of women's lives have both been transformed enough so that it is no longer possible to pretend that the impulses to dominate, aggress or sexually exploit others are "male" urges alone.'

One of the many areas Wolf deals with is 'the feminine fear of power'. As one example she shows how sport can define early in women's lives how they are trained to respond – or not – to issues later in life. 'In contrast to the methods of boys' sports teams, girls' social organisation is profoundly subjective and undemocratic. The "system of government" girls learn in the playground ranges from a popularity oligarchy to an Evita-type personality cult that is, at best, a benign dictatorship.' While many girls, particularly at single-sex schools, excel at sports and are applauded by their peers, this is not the norm for most.

47

'Unlike boys' athletic leaders, whose achievement can be measured objectively and whose prominence can be grudgingly accepted by less athletic boys as being "just" physical, leaders of girls' groups reign on the unmerited basis of charisma, looks, clothes, popularity – that is, on the basis of a rudimentary celebrity. Girls learn that leadership is subjective, shaky, undeserved and personal. They can have little sense that a good leader can bring the whole group triumph and cohesiveness.'

Here, you feel a momentary surge of triumph since women in this state have a raft of terrific role models, from the President to Mary Harney. We all know that the women who achieve in a visible way and are suitably rewarded for it are usually better, work harder, often look better and take greater risks than the majority. But this can compound a feeling of inadequacy among the hordes of women who are doing terrific jobs without necessarily getting the Oscars.

'Playground lessons mean that women lack a working model of female meritocracy,' writes Wolf. 'Until recently it was marriage rather than achievement that determined a woman's rise in the world; women saw other women getting ahead on the basis of their beauty or sexuality. This old corruption of female meritocracy is compounded by the way the media today attribute women achievers' status to their looks or to a husband, male relative or male mentor.'

How we get the male powerbrokers to accept women as equals is addressed by Wolf in a pragmatic, readable way. In summary, she advises us to adopt and adapt new psychological strategies. Many are those that men have been using successfully for years. They have worked for them. They can work for women.

She shows that women do not have to get on with each other, to like each other or to agree with each other – the old notion of sisterhood. 'The women's groups that self-destruct today do so because they are structured for consensus; because they encourage a style of speech that places the question "what hurts?" at its centre, rather than "what can be done?" Women have been taught to believe they have to like each other and work through their differences instead of working with them.

'In its new phase, feminism must begin to utilise the only substance strong enough to forge coalitions from the diverse agendas of those who constitute the majority: mutual self-interest, bolstered by impersonal self-respect.'

Wolf is a treat. She is not only thinking. She is telling you what to do. It is the ABC of the new agenda that puts her way ahead of the pack. With regard to how men and women with power behave, she shows how the male experience works better.

'It is not men with power who behave, generally, in individualistic, defensively competitive ways – it is the few women who tend to do so, misunderstanding what is really going on in the subterranean dynamics of the culture in which they find themselves.'

How do men at the top with power behave, she asks, then answers, 'They pass it around to their friends.'

You get the message? This is just a flavour of *Fire with Fire*. My advice to Grace was to go out, buy it and read it immediately. She said she would like to get in contact with other women in a similar situation to herself, so that they could meet and exchange views. Without consulting Wolf, I think this could be a good idea if they began with a positive agenda like how they could benefit from one another's experiences, swap information and useful contacts. But *not* if they used it to berate the long-gone husbands and carry on sobbing. If anybody wants to contact Grace, they can write to me and mark the envelope 'Grace' in the left-hand corner.

This is not the end of Naomi Wolf. With her first book, *The Beauty Myth*, she established herself. One of her biggest successes was not just in invigorating the 1970s feminists who had begun to falter, but in getting a whole new following among young women who yawned and groaned at the word 'feminism'. Her much-vaunted good looks probably have something to do with this – although they have equally alienated many critics who are envious of her youth, glowing skin and tumbling hair.

I like beautiful people and if they talk sense, it is even better. If they talk and write like Naomi Wolf, you have the best of all worlds.

1 February 1994

EURO-ELECTION 1994

*It amazes me that women still allow themselves to be
seduced into hostile structures like political parties without laying down new ground rules.*

Will *realpolitik* for women in the 1990s mean that the long-
serving party members will continue to make the tea and
lick the envelopes in the backrooms – the only difference
being that now they will be fetching and carrying for the
celebrity women flown in over their heads?

Will they have to be clever/handsome/articulate and a
household name before they even consider running for a
seat in politics? Is the upcoming Euro-election in danger
of being labelled the Miss Europe Contest? Have the women
– either those with long service in political parties seeking
their just reward or the well known women who are being
sought to fill the gender gap – stopped to think who is
pulling the strings? Will they do the foot-slogging and
leafleting? Will the canvasser on the doorstep tell the
punters how the 'name' woman on the ticket will do the
job much better than she could herself? Yet again, are the
women to blame? Should the women accept the guilt for
not making it yet again? Were they timid for far too long?

This week has seen a new phenomenon in Irish politics.
Women, who have been marginalised or outright ignored
since the foundation of the state, are suddenly in fashion.
They are being headhunted for jobs that were previously

almost the exclusive preserve of men. Until the early 1980s, nearly all the women elected to the Dáil and Seanad were widows, daughters or other relations of male politicians. The women's movement shafted in a new layer of women without any overt political connections. Garret FitzGerald's leadership attracted some. Others were drawn to the Progressive Democrats, which had Mary Harney in a pivotal role. The Labour Party attracted strong, bright and stoical women who were loyal to a fault; to such a fault that they hung in there for decades with little or no reward. When Eithne FitzGerald made history and headlines by winning her seat in Dublin South last year with almost two quotas, she had been in the party for more than twenty years and had been a member of Dublin County Council for some twelve years.

But before the general election in November 1993, the Labour Party had no woman in the Dáil or Seanad. Neither had Democratic Left. It was that election that made the party bosses sit up and take notice. They had seen President Robinson elected, but it was when women forged through in unforeseen numbers that they began to get the wind up. Fianna Fáil just got its five sitting women back. Fine Gael lost one. Democratic Left elected Liz McManus and the PDs got the highest percentage gain, with four women out of its ten elected TDs.

The parties in the Republic do not do their own internal polling. If they did, they could have expected the eruption. For years the polls in Britain have been telling all the parties that women are seen as more credible candidates. They are seen as more honest, hard-working and sincere. Those polls also showed that women's voting patterns were different from men's; women tended to vote for personalities. They were volatile and generally had few hang-ups about switching parties at election time. Neither did women cast their votes lightly.

These facts were evident in the November 1992 general election in Ireland. What was immediately obvious to all the parties was that they needed women immediately. What was also obvious was that they did not have enough women. And since then most, except Fianna Fáil, have done little to trawl for prospective candidates. Now Fianna Fáil has set up women's branches in each of the forty-one constituencies. This makes one realise why that party is still the largest in the State.

But Fianna Fáil apparently failed to realise that while it was boosting its members' self-esteem, coaching them for office, a lot of the timidity and lack of confidence were disappearing also. The result showed this week when furious Fianna Fáil women went public with their grievances over the selection for the European elections. They were as good as the rest, they felt, but if they were not, there were women such as Marian McGennis, who were.

After the selection of Olive Braiden as Fianna Fáil Euro-candidate, Ms McGennis told this reporter that she was 'relieved' at the outcome. She wanted to concentrate on building up a strong national profile and getting more involved in domestic politics. To date, her Seanad performance is impressive. She also admired Ms Braiden, she said, and believed that Fianna Fáil would gain immensely with her as a member.

Senior Fianna Fáil sources say that the European elections are different from national ones. They say a different type of candidate runs for Europe – that the real blood and guts of politics are fought out in the Dáil. That could be right. But if right, it should mean that Fianna Fáil should be jetting in 'name' men also.

The same wounded feelings are evident in Labour and Fine Gael. Labour Councillor Bernie Malone, who has been waiting to step into Barry Desmond's seat, will now be up against Orla Guerin. Ms Malone is well-known within the party and within her own Dublin patch, but she would not appear to stand much chance against Ms Guerin, who has been in the sitting rooms of the nation almost daily for a couple of years, doing excellent and award-winning coverage of eastern Europe.

The PDs, one of whose members also approached Ms Braiden, tend to take the moral high ground on their number of elected women, but they also have egg on their collective face. In 1987 they imposed Geraldine Kennedy, already a well known journalist and now this newspaper's political correspondent, on Helen Keogh's constituency in Dun Laoghaire, to the grassroots' disgust. The rumours are rampant and 'who asked who' is becoming increasingly unclear. If all the names that have been mooted and mentioned and sanctioned make it to Europe, the Irish MEPs could well be the toast of the continent.

Even though she has apparently rejected Fianna Fáil's advances, Marian Finucane could be there. So could Adi Roche, the Cork anti-nuclear campaigner. Polly Devlin has been mentioned. For the PDs? Eimear Haughey was talked about. Several other women's names are being trotted out – and this in a country which says it cannot find enough qualified women to put in some time on its ferociously difficult County Enterprise Boards?

The most important feature of this phenomenon is that many of the cleverest and most politicised women in the country do not seem to realise that they are getting moved up for one reason – because the men need them. Women are needed to fill the seats being left vacant by the men of whom the public have tired. Women are still the puppets.

12 February 1994

WHO IS BERNIE MALONE?

This is one story behind the reality of the way men work when they decide to allow women into their clubs, pubs and parties. Only by their rules, they insist. Bernie Malone MEP is a classic case of one woman who fought them and won.

From the party that gave you President Mary Robinson, take a look at what the Irish Labour Party is now doing with another highly political woman, Bernie Malone.

From the party that went on a focused rampage against Fianna Fáil and its so-called lack of morality and its alleged glut of opportunism in the last Dáil, look at what it is now doing to Bernie Malone.

For every woman who thinks about how she casts her vote, look carefully at the Labour Party and its record on Bernie Malone. For Bernie Malone, you can read its attitude to yourself and every other woman.

From the party that flagged President Robinson in her mid-forties as 'young', describes Dick Spring and all the middle-aged men as 'young', the message that is coming through about Bernie Malone is that at forty-five she is 'old'. Remember that when you vote.

Except for one comment from a high-profile TD in another party, everything I heard about Bernie Malone before I met her was negative, coy or forgettable. They ranged from, 'she lacks gravitas' to 'she has no profile'. Others, who like to think they have a monopoly on pol.

cred., wagged earnest fingers and lectured. 'You have to realise that nobody knows her. Who is Bernie Malone? You should know that she would never hold Barry Desmond's seat. What has she done?'

The TD (who does not want to be named) said: 'Bernie Malone? She was a very important role model for me. Back in 1986 when she was the first woman chair of Dublin County Council – at a time when I had no political ambitions – I thought: "Hey, there's a woman who is head of something important". That registered with me. It has always stayed in my mind.'

Now that I've had a few meetings with her over a few days, I think Bernie Malone is shrewd, witty, thoughtful, philosophical, realistic, steeped in politics and unbelievably idealistic after twenty years of the swinging fortunes of the Labour Party – the party that has just seemingly pushed her to one side. Worse, it seems to have distanced itself from her. It is providing little support for her European election campaign, even though she is now the sitting MEP, having recently taken over Barry Desmond's seat on his appointment to the European Court of Auditors. When the issue of the elections comes up, it is staggering how many senior party figures (many who whine endlessly on about feminism and equality) can manage to avoid even mentioning her name.

The collective wisdom of the clutter of Wise Boys who run the party decided that the talented journalist Orla Guerin would deliver the goods for them. She may. She may not. If she does not, it will not be for want of effort from HQ. Ministers and other senior party figures are smoothing Guerin's path and whistling up all the media coverage at their command.

Last week, when Malone's own car was playing up, she had to look to family and friends for lifts to constituency meetings, while the boys and girls with titles swept Guerin along in their Volvos or Peugeots. What the Wise Boys do not seem to have taken into account is that their tactics are straight out of the catalogue of What-Men-Should-Have-Learned-To-Forget. Their tactics are also straight down the line against their famous Killarney conference when they were on a roll and trotted out all sorts of heady promises – among them that they would actively promote their own women to share the spoils. This was when it was easy to be different. Their women colleagues, who are going along with the new-age revisionism, seem to have forgotten what it was like to be alone and isolated for so long. Was it for this that a record number of Labour women were elected to the Dáil? To learn how to do it the boys' way?

Back to Bernie Malone who, while aware of all this, is still infinitely loyal. From time to time, she uses the words 'wounded' or 'hurt' to describe her feelings. She and her husband Frank, who introduced her to Labour Party politics, run their own joint solicitor's practice in Portmarnock. They have been married for over twenty years. They do not have children.

She was elected to Dublin County Council in 1979 and has a fine record on issues such as rezoning and travellers. One of a large family, she talks about Dublin in the way real Dubs do – as if there is nowhere like it in the world. Is she gravitas-less? She considers. 'I was elected to the council by people who knew me. They voted me back again and again. If the party wanted a different profile, I could work it up.'

She has a devastatingly simple approach to the myth-ridden world of politics. She has always worked extremely hard, has missed a Dáil seat a couple of times, was refused a nomination to the Seanad even though she told those-who-are-supposed-to-be-wise that it would be a good platform for Europe. In spite of all this, she has no intention of leaving the party. 'Of course not. If I am selected, I will fight; if not, I will carry on anyway.'

Does this come from some profound philosophical view of the world and politics? She giggles. No way. She moves from challenge to challenge. Now it is the selection convention. After that it will be the election. Either way, she will campaign during the election. The party is the most important thing. The party is more important than the leadership.

She speaks simply and sincerely. It is her life; her family, she adds.

But she does question the way the party is going. Is it now going to be a two-lane thing – one lane for the workers and another for the outsiders who will blow in at the last minute and claim the plaudits? She says it slowly, questioningly. She simply wants to know. She is also cautious in what she is telling me. I have to strap together bits and pieces of information from a variety of sources. It would make a good mini-series.

Malone was well aware that the top brass in the Labour Party did not take her seriously. She knew they were headhunting. Then came the bombshell about Orla Guerin, the week before last.

Apparently, Dick Spring saw the parliamentary party separately and in groups. Initially, none of them would tell Bernie Malone who the outsider was. She was summoned to see Spring in the Berkeley Court Hotel. Brendan Howlin, who was with him, kissed her, continental-style, on both cheeks – apparently not something he usually does. Dick Spring told her the news.

Did she feel like cracking a heavy vase over their heads? Again, Malone is cautious. She says: 'No. They felt badly about it. I know they did.'

And despite the body language she has been getting from former colleagues – 'They turn away, to one side, when they see you' – Malone says firmly: 'The party has a lot of very highly principled people in it. The PDs claim the high moral ground but I am proud of the Labour Party and most of the people in it.'

Is she mad or does she possess some odd kind of personality that would seem to be at odds with politics as commonly practised? She laughs. 'I don't know. I'm not going to be analysed. I don't want to go into therapy. I suppose (in family law) I'm used to being intuitive and empathic. Maybe that's a failure in a politician?'

22 February 1994

Mother's Fools' Day

So many people said this was a new low – or high? – in
cynicism; their reactions made me extremely happy.

If anything is likely to make mothers feel like real fools, it
is Mother's Day. It drips with condescension, coyness,
vulgarity and plain lies.

Mother's Day is such a stupid day. Like *reel stoopid*, as
they say Stateside. Or *stup-a*, as they say in Dublin. Or *naff*,
as they say in Neasden and Stillorgan. I never heard of it
until I became a mother nineteen years ago, and promptly
forbade anybody to say or do anything about it.

For me, it is not an item. It crawls in slyly in the middle
of the mid-term break, pancakes, International Women's
Day, St Patrick's Day, Good Friday, Easter, First Com-
munions and Confirmations – all the events that are
organised, controlled, worked for and sweated over by
mothers. Even if you want to avoid it, it is hard to miss the
rows of arch, coquettish, flirtatious, kittenish and skittish
cards (in Easons last week they ranged in price from 40p
to the satin-lined ones at about £6) lining the shelves in
your local shop – below the Easter eggs that will be down
at eye-level next week. Do not be fooled by the messages,
flowers or perfume. Your husband does not love you to
eternal distraction, nor do your children. If you belong to
either of those groups who swear eternal fealty to the *bean
an tí* on one day of the year, you should cop on.

If your mother went AWOL in the morning, you would grieve. There would be no one to give you the cod liver oil, glistening shirt, bleached boxer shorts, cornflakes, or dust the dandruff off your collar. There would be no hot dinner in the evening. The rings around the bath would just grow blacker and greasier. The smears on the windows would eventually block out the world and there would be no money for Christmas, because no one would have joined the local savings club in September. That, mothers, is the reality of your existence while the patriarchy continues to rule. But just to keep you happy, to make you feel you are special, the patriarchs dreamed up the notion of (apparently) giving you one day off in the year. Is there any other job where you get *one day* off work? In that one day you get to avoid cooking the breakfast, dinner and tea. You might be taken out to lunch – most restaurants in Dublin and around the country are booked solid for tomorrow. But is it not sheer black humour that they slotted the day into a Sunday?

Most Sundays are a bit laid back anyway. You sweat over the stove, make cool sandwiches to keep the in-laws happy when they call in the afternoon and try to detach yourself from their veiled jibes when you apologise that the kids got to the cake-tin first. You are used to it. And if you are lucky you might get to flick through the newspapers while himself takes the family off for a few hours. Just an average Sunday.

Tomorrow, though, will be different. You will be Mother for the day. You will have to look surprised/happy/over-the-moon when the gang throws you a few bits of burnt toast and cold tea. Then they will take you out when you have cleaned up the mess. You will look like an eejity 1950s bride on the first night when you are landed in the eaterie, probably surrounded by many more lookalikes. You will still have to juggle the spoon down Baby's throat because the gang never learned to do that. You will have to change Baby in the women's room – I am offering £10 to the first man who can prove he has ever campaigned for changing facilities in the men's room. You will still have to soothe the fretful cranks on the way home. You will probably end up putting them to bed because all the heavy sighing has got too much. You will pass out, thankful it is all over for another year.

Are you receiving loud and clear, mothers of Ireland? If you spend your time convincing yourself you have a great job, tomorrow will convince you of the indignity of your situation. You do a terrific job for no pay, with no set hours, little time off and no holidays. Mother's Day only highlights the deficiencies of your station in life.

12 March 1994

THE ALLURE OF THE ROARING ROYALS

Another blip in the lives of Charles and Di. Another chip at fantasy; more real than Dallas *at its height and as compulsively awful to watch as read about.*

What do Fianna Fáil TD Eoin Ryan and Dame Barbara Cartland have in common? They both think that the British royals should get their act together and realise that they are working for a business – a sort of UK plc – which brings in millions of tourists and pounds every year.

This was a week in which almost everyone I spoke to had an opinion on Charles and Di. Most were sympathetic to him after publication of his biography, which is being serialised in the *Sunday Times.* As with the assassination of JFK, most could remember where they were when they watched the royal wedding. It seems to have brought a sort of Mills and Boonish tear of sentiment to the eyes of the most cynical. I remember watching the glass coach, the pomp and ceremony, in Kerry. Charles Flanagan, Fine Gael TD for Laois–Offaly, and member of the Oireachtas Women's Rights Committee, recalls that he was at home and 'everyone in the house was glued to it'. He now sees the couple as 'two pathetic individuals', with Charles in a no-win situation. They were rushed into marriage and were then forced to play out their relationship in a goldfish bowl. 'People can talk about the damage to the monarchy but I see it as a great human tragedy.'

Prince Charles 'is either trying to set the record straight or to evoke public sympathy. Perhaps he would have been better to crawl away from the thing. Diana has obviously been to the depths of despair and back over the years. It is tragic. They seem to have everything in life except enjoyment,' says Flanagan.

Jonathan Dimbleby's biography, *The Prince of Wales*, has generally received vitriolic attacks in Britain, with the media variously accusing the heir to the throne of self-pity, of building on his 'wimp' image, of throwing serious doubt on his judgement and his suitability to be king.

Communications guru and managing director of Carr Communications, Terry Prone – who tutors the high and mighty as well as those ambitious for top jobs on how to control and manage their public images – says categorically: 'I would *never* advise someone to do what Prince Charles has done. There is a dread seduction about the word "openness"; people can use it to put a positive cast on what is sometimes little more than promiscuous abandonment of privacy.'

Maura Wall Murphy, co-ordinator of the Family Mediation Service, sees the Andrew Morton book on Princess Diana and Dimbleby's book on Prince Charles thus: 'The message coming loud and clear from these two books is of two people who are desperate for understanding. They are each saying, "Please try to understand me, please see my point of view".' Ms Wall Murphy says this is a common reaction of couples who turn up seeking mediation. 'They are each saying: "I'm not a bad person. I'm trying my best".'

They each have a desperate need to be understood and for people to listen to their side of the story. They are usually coming from different perspectives.

She sees Princess Diana as a woman of enormous compassion with a real gift for communicating with people. 'She's a natural. I could see her as a social worker or a therapist – and she would make a very good one.' Charles? 'Maybe he should be an artist or something in that field.'

Falling in love is only a 'short-term' stage in a relationship and many couples come to marriage with very different expectations. 'In the case of Diana, she was coming with very unequal power – in age, education and maturity. She was an adolescent growing into adulthood. He had years of experience of the protocol surrounding the role, while she had none. Their roles were dominant, not the relationship. It is not helpful to take sides, for them or their children. Maybe there are lessons to be learned about marriage. Maybe this is a purification of the monarchy. Maybe it needed to be examined.'

She adds that there is little point in blaming the parents. 'Most parents do the best they can in the only way they know how. Partners in a marriage bring the baggage of their family of origin.'

This is supported by Dr Evelyn Quinn, lecturer in psychology at UCD, who compares the upbringing of children in the past. 'Whole generations were reared in Ireland and elsewhere in a cruel fashion. Coldness between parents and children was typical.' She cites John Watson, a psychologist who was very influential in the US in the 1920s. His message was that it was very wrong to cuddle your children, that it would encourage 'ineffective behaviours'. Ms Wall Murphy says Diana needed her friends to help her grow up within the marriage as well as the advice of palace officials. The result was inevitable, she feels. 'And as soon as someone begins to fight out in anger against a terrible situation, they're labelled mad or bad.'

Many of Terry Prone's views echo Maura Wall Murphy's, although they are coming from different perspectives.

Ms Prone says: 'One of the problems here is that the two participants seem to be playing a PR game against each other – trying not to solve problems but to create a public persona they can read about and feel justified by. Playing the PR game with your private life as feedstuff is like keeping a tiger in the back garden – hellish exciting but ultimately deadly. Before I would advise a public figure to authorise a book or give in-depth, nakedly personal interviews, I would want them to be clear on the end objective. What do they want to achieve? Too often they just want "to get it off their chest". Express their anger. There is a myth that expressed anger solves problems and frees people to make progress. Garbage. Expressed anger leads to more anger. Nobody solves any problems (other than selling books and newspapers) and innocent bystanders, such as offspring, tend to get side-swiped.'

He who lives by the PR sword often dies by it, says Terry Prone. She cites a chapter in the book where Prince Charles talks about his father. 'While the prince interprets his father's attitude (to wed Diana or give her up) as an ultimatum, Prone says this shows much more about Charles than his father.

'It says that the prince is a man prepared to use his low self-esteem as a justification for actions taken or not taken. It says he has autonomy but refuses to use it and retrospectively lays off blame on others. He (Charles) comes very badly out of the extracts so far. His sacrifice of his friends to the pressures allegedly exerted by his wife is unconscionable.'

Olive Braiden, director of the Dublin Rape Crisis Centre, says the image of Charles in the Dimbleby book is one of 'a very damaged person'. Such people are unable to offer much in a relationship, particularly marriage. Their own hurt prevents them from helping anybody else. Several factors contribute to the continuance of the hurt, such as where they come in the family. Princess Anne's strong personality and bond with her father did not help her brother, says Braiden.

Eoin Ryan does not care a fig for the personalities of the royal family and their endless traumas and troubles. However, when he went to his local newsagent last Sunday, the *Sunday Times* at the new price of 50p was sold out. 'I thought it could be very bad for the Irish papers if these guys are going to dump their 50p newspapers with "puller" stories here. That is worrying.'

30 October 1994

Reversal of Fortunes

*Down with all dictators of fashion which make women
feel bad, sad, beautiful, ugly or worthwhile just because
of their shape.*

Fat is fast becoming a feminist issue. Again. While there
are women out there preparing for Christmas by swapping
diets and denuding bookshelves of X, Y, or Z-Plans on how
to look like Kate Moss, there is a critical mass who are
saying, 'I'm fat as hell and I'm not going to take it any
more.'

'It' is the welter of propaganda that turns women into
moping melancholics if they will not fit into last year's ski-
pants. And that ballyhoo is so strongly promoted by
advertising and the media generally that you would be hard-
pressed to think of any woman other than Roseanne Barr
on TV or in public life who is not a size ten or twelve,
fourteen at a pinch. Even the women who will not take the
money from Marty Whelan in the detergent ads – who
presumably are supposed to be your average Ms Housewife
– are stick-insects compared with the real thing. So good
on you, Lorelei Harris, for your programme that went out
yesterday afternoon on RTE Radio 1 and will be repeated
next Monday at 8.30 pm. It is called *Dreaming of Fat Men*.

Briefly, it is four fat women at a dinner party who
salivate over the dishes in front of them. They let rip about
their fatness. They describe some of the drawbacks. But

these are no whinging women. They whoop with lusty laughter. They giggle at themselves. They talk about their layers of adipose tissue with spluttering abandon. They dissect life with the same precision with which they attack their oysters. Theirs is no squalid affair with a few extra roast potatoes and a tincture of cream with the fruit salad. It has all the sounds of a feast of Bacchanalian proportions.

This is the first programme I have ever heard that celebrates fatness in women. They are not trying to change themselves. One says if she had one wish she would ask to have a prettier face. Another talks about the discos and other places of entertainment she would not go to because of her size. So she ends up ballroom dancing with people twenty years her senior because she is accepted there. Other side-issues of fatness, such as getting clothes to fit them or a man to love them, are dealt with in a strictly analytical way.

These are no victim women. They never talk about wanting to be like Kate Moss. At most, they might want to be accepted as shapely, but they know they are not going to be. They are going to be fat for most of their lives.

'I'm fat and fabulous. I am big, cuddly, sexy, delicious. I'm a French cream-filled pastry with a drizzle of dark chocolate. That's on a good day,' says one, and erupts into waves of belly laughter. These are sensual women who are not afraid to say that their love of food probably has something to do with deprivation in other parts of their lives. With some it relates back to childhood. With others there are short poignant pieces where their bruised self-images rise to the surface over the clatter of plates, bellowing laughter and descriptions of themselves as big women, voluptuous women, Rubenesque women or Junoesque.

One of the women was followed by a man who persistently asked her out to lunch. Then she found out he was a 'chubby-chaser'. She was angry and frustrated. It reinforced her dream of having a man who wants her in spite of her build – the woman she is. 'Sometimes I love the way I look. Sometimes I catch glimpses of myself in a store window and I say, "Wow, that's a great-looking woman". Sometimes I wake up in the morning and look in the mirror and say, "Why, why did I binge last night?" '

One had 'life-modelled' for art students. A smart-ass at the back of the class had drawn a picture of the back of a bus. Her tone was withering. You have to imagine a lot with this programme. Radio at its best.

Harris's programme comes at a time when a 'Fat is beautiful, fat is normal' movement is taking off in Britain and probably elsewhere. It is an inevitable reaction to the boom of models who are called 'super' mainly because of the amount of money they command and the gang of well-known men they swing off on their way to somewhere glitzy. But there is bubbling trouble brewing for these starlets of the 1980s and 1990s. The fashion designers are ganging up on them and threatening to get Henriettas from Ohio and Honoras from Idaho for a tenth of the price, who could do the job just as well. They are fed up with the super-tantrums, the super moody whims of the 'I have a face, a bony-assed body and I can sell your clothes' breed who have replaced royals and real stars in the society pages.

They pout as often as possible, seldom smile and have run Brigitte Bardot and other classy dames out of San Tropez by cluttering it up with their chunky jewellery, funky followers and matchbox duplexes where they have their mommas and poppas staying over. *Mon Dieu.*

In Britain, two women called Stephanie and Fay run Positive Plus Sizes (PPS) which got going because of the numbers of Afro-Caribbean and other black women who come from cultures which believe that the fatter you are, the healthier you are. They and others are fearful of the advertising and social pressure on such women to confirm to the 'white' norm of skin and bone and chewing carrots . . . and carrots . . . and carrots. Stephanie and Fay, who are both winners of the Big and Beautiful contest, run classes to reinforce the confidence of black women.

A University of Arizona survey found that young black girls have an infinitely more positive image of themselves. In a survey of two hundred and fifty teenagers, 90 per cent of white girls were dissatisfied with their bodies, while 70 per cent of blacks were satisfied and were not into dieting. The white girls' emphasis was on thinness, while the blacks spoke about shapeliness.

All of this mania for thinness is still relatively new in rural Ireland where a woman was defined as attractive by being 'a fine strapping girl'. The reasons ranged from the commercial – all the better to plough the land, to milk the cows, to rear large families – to the health factor. When I was growing up in the 1950s and 1960s it was still not unusual for parents to worry if a daughter was losing weight. The scourge of TB was still too recent in folk memory for it not to be the first image that sprang to mind if you were off your food or if you were conscious of having a big backside.

Not only is Lorelei Harris's programme compulsive listening, it also raises many other issues that apply to women. As one of the women says: 'A man is never called fat. He is solid, strong, big and powerful, while a woman is weak-willed. A fat woman is not looked on as a woman or a sexual object.'

They may well be surprised. This programme opens a can or worms – or a carton of clotted cream – that may not quickly go away.

10 November 1994

LIFE ON THE EDGE

Most women create the daily lives for their families to function at their best in. But it's the feast days that really nearly drive them to sticking their heads rather than the turkeys in the oven.

It is time to ditch the famous Superwoman motto: 'Life is too short to stuff a mushroom,' and coin a new one running along the lines of: 'Stuff Superwoman and get real'. And for the week that is in it, the most apposite slogan is, 'Life is too short to stuff turkeys.' Let the breeders teach the turkeys to stuff themselves. Or let the sellers stuff them for you.

Next year will be the twentieth anniversary of the publication of Shirley Conran's book that became the bible of the barely-liberated generation of women in the late 1960s and early 1970s. Conran got herself into the big time with her challenging mottoes about mushrooms and zippy epigrams like, 'No one can make washing-up sensuous'. The book became a sensation and sales went into space. All those who took it seriously have been paying the price ever since.

What it actually did was to build on the entirely new conspiracy which taught women to put up with juggling two jobs – one paid (outside the home) and another unpaid (inside). Conran was one of the shapers of a couple of generations of women who go around with smiles plastered on their made-up or made-over faces while inside they are quivering on the edge of a nervous breakdown. What it did was to send out another snotty Hampstead-ish message – that real women actually were doing daft things like stuffing mushrooms. That it was posh to turn the business of cooking into something called cuisine. That real women could be both a Doris Day in an apron and a Bacall or a Redgrave-type queening it over a salon of talking heads.

Despite the fact that I had never seen or heard of anybody stuffing a mushroom until I read that book, the truth is that nearly twenty years on, women are still cooking meals, cleaning the houses, ironing his 'n' her shirts, paying a char and worrying about the minder. This week, they are sending the change-of-mind letters to Santy. Many are also trying to make it to the boardroom with their smart briefcases and wrinkle-free suits. Some have new-men spouses – some are saints, others are barely satisfactory and the majority are just edging on minimal. Taking the kids swimming or to Croke Park or soccer-rugby places, picking them up from the minder or taking them to McDonald's for their tea to give mammy a break. Break, my eye. It's so that she can give the whole house a good clean or cook twenty freezer dinners for the coming week.

Superwoman and her sisters taught us a whole variety of tricks for making the job-in-the-home less of a hassle. I remember one bit which described the number of things you could take upstairs at the same time; the number of things you could do when you were there, and the number of things you could bring down in one trip. This was to drastically cut down the 2.3 – or was it 23? – miles a day it was reckoned that women spent walking around the house doing the housework. One of the few things of any worth was the gimmick telling you how to defrost the freezer with a hairdryer in double-quick time – if you don't electrocute yourself in the process. It was all about apparently efficient rush and bustle that gave you time to get out to work and put on a dinner for madding crowds and still left you time to soak in scented baths, keep your mate randy and read Beatrix Potter to the kids.

The false smiles and unseen quivers persist year-round for most high-achieving women with kids. But this week they are into overdrive. This week the majority of working mothers are in a spin of frazzle and hassle. They are combing shops for toys and food. They are trying to catch office parties and drinks dos. They are working against the siege mentality which creeps up at this festival, as if the world will close down for a month or the President will drop in for a cup of tea. Or just to impress peers and in-laws. Hence a mix of over-full freezers and a flurry of spring cleaning at midnight. I have not joined up with Nora Bennis and taken on her philosophy of keeping women at home all day, every day, until the kids are reared. Whatever that age might be. More serious consideration of the split lives of working mothers came up recently in the course of an ICTU seminar on media skills, organised by Margaret Nolan, equality officer and Oliver Donohoe, research and development officer, for some of their women officials.

Cynthia Ní Mhurchú, easily one of the most efficient and professional of the women working in RTE, gave a superb and pithy overview of where women figure in the national broadcasting station. She had facts and figures from a number of sources. They were frightening. I was not as well prepared as her but from personal experience was able to show that the same applies to women in the print media.

While women have high visibility on the box or on the pages of newspapers, they have damn all input at the level of policy or decision-making. And the few women who make it to the top rarely help other women get up the ladder. We all agreed that not only do women not support each other, neither do they promote each other in the way that men do from the cradle up. 'I know just the guy you need' . . . 'he's sound' . . . or 'He's dead on, that guy.' It works. We can see the result.

The end result of women not doing this is equally obvious. And it is one of the main reasons why half the population out there are wondering why stories about women's lives rarely make the news; why things like men's sports are gradually dominating at least one of the national airwaves all year round instead of seasonally, why mediocre men are thrown on programmes to 'balance out' brilliant women and why women in the news are usually portrayed as victims or vixens.

It was a bit of an eye-opener for the trade unionists – even though many of them have fairly regular contact with the media – and it started a vigorous debate. Some admitted afterwards that they had changed their views that women like Ní Mhurchú, myself and other women in the media had let them down. They agreed to monitor more carefully and to lobby more. And since Shirley Conran was one of those who started it all, I suggest that this Christmas Day, you throw Superwoman in the range – all the better to roast the turkey – while you play with the kids' toys. If he can't cope, get a take-away.

22 December 1994

DO NOT FORGET – EVER

The power-play of men is about the only thing that is getting more transparent and is more visible. Whether women turn them off or tell them to feck off is another matter.

Before you get further into 1995, look back in anger. Look back to the recent past when the new government allowed itself to create an extra Minister of State (Pat Rabbitte) just to make their numbers add up to a power quota.

For years these men have been serving up platitudes to women about gender quotas. These same men have often said that such quotas are not necessary. We/you can work it out, they said. Or they have paid lip-service to 60/40 quotas in politics. Lip-service was, and is, the height of it. You now have the living proof that if they want anything badly enough they can get it. They can make or break laws. They can pull fast ones very fast. Or they can sit on the fences. Forever.

Look back in anger at the fact that not one of the negotiators to form this new government was a woman. They will say they had women on the sidelines, as cheer-leaders/cautioners/comforters. They had the women up front fielding the flak from the media. Then as soon as John, Dick and Proinsias were swathed in their technicolour dreamcoat, they pulled up the anchor of the ark and let the women swim like hell – for the shore or to pull themselves aboard.

In the year of 1995, just under five years short of the year 2,000, get the message fast: these men do not give a damn about you and your female nitpickings. They look and sound pompously OK when required, but once your back is turned they nod and wink and throw their eyes up to heaven. Thank God that's over for now, they say, and go home to throw more soiled underwear at the wife. Look at the present inquisition of the former Fianna Fáil Ministers. Do you hear a woman's voice asking a question? You do not. And all parties are culpable. Despite the fact that the single shining star of the Dáil ding-dong before Christmas was Mary Harney – and acknowledged as such by the entire chamber as well as most of the country – why is Des O'Malley now playing with all the boys? Since his leader proved her mettle in the most difficult forum, without notes or scripts, showing her skill at oratory laced with wit and passion – where is she now when her surgical skill at probing the tumours is sorely needed?

If anybody needed proof of Mary Harney's popularity ratings in that period, they should have been in my usually sober bank in College Green on Thursday, 15 December. The Dáil was coming live over the tedious business of borrowing off Peter to pay Paul. When Mary Harney rose, so did all heads, from the struggle of form-filling, juggling overdrafts or smugly putting a few bob in against a rainy day. From the highest floor-walker to the shortest manager to the most indigent customer, faces lightened up. Smiles broke out and spirits rose.

In that period, if Mary Harney had declared herself as

a candidate for a new job as National Ombud *(sic* – it's a Norwegian gender-neutral word which we have corrupted) to run the country and keep tabs on the entire silly lot of them, would there have been one voice of dissent? She could still go for it and win. So you can pass over the PDs' leader when you look back in anger. But do not be deflected. Look back at the single extra junior ministry this Government has given to women. So now there are four instead of three – two senior and two juniors.

Look back in anger to the fact that not one woman is yet secretary of a government department – even in Equality and Law Reform. Look at the figures which show that all the donkey work in these departments is done by women clerical workers who are paid a pittance. The entire system would grind to a halt without them but does anybody think about that when they are drawing up their budgets? Imagine the scene. What would a minister, any minister, do without a clear script to read from? What would he do without a diligent woman to keep track of his social/personal/working life? He would not survive the next election. That is what he would do.

Look back in anger to the exceptionally few women who are principals of schools while the vast majority of teachers are women. Look in anger at the health services where all but a very few of the top jobs in medicine are held by men. Look at the churches where women are invisible on the front lines.

Look back in anger at all the women who are still getting beaten up by spouses, sons, brothers or just strangers. Look back at the legal system that still puts a raped woman into the witness box without the benefit of her own solicitor or barrister and proceeds to question her as if she were the criminal. Look at all the women who are still beavering away in their own time to raise money to build more refuges to contain the women victims of these thugs. Look at these thugs; they are still well regarded by many of their peers who think what they're doing is not such a bad thing. If men do *not* think like this, let them prove it. One way is to turn the law around so that the refuges are for the criminal men, thus leaving the battered women and children in their own homes.

Look at all the powerful jobs held by men – many of them jaded, old and grey men who still have the crassness to assume they are somewhere near to God in wisdom and I-know-bestness.

Look back in anger at the number of men who front your television screens and radio programmes. Is there one woman's voice to be heard, apart from a couple of newsreaders, until after lunch most days? This week saw the start of yet another b-o-r-ing and incredibly stupid show given to Gerry Ryan on television. How many does that make?

You do not have to look very far back in anger to realise that you are a fool if you let these boys' clubs dominate your lives. Let them know it. Let the anger sizzle. Then let the polls show them. Let the ratings drop to the zeros they deserve.

12 January 1995

WIFIE

This is all about what can happen if you marry an ambitious man. As his wife, you will be expected to stay in the kitchen with him and still face the fire of begrudgery outside.

There are quaint old Irish traditions. And there are super-wives. No connection, you would assume, since super-wives have not yet hit these shores with anything like the long-lensed intensity they enjoy or suffer in other Western countries, notably the United States, more recently in Britain.

But you would assume in vain. Take one famous Irishism: 'Would you like to be buried with my people?' And then take Cherie Blair, an independent woman, well-educated, well-connected, well-heeled and highly articulate. She is the wife of Tony Blair, the newish, high profile leader of the British Labour Party on whom the hopes of his followers are pinned to take them out of (almost) permanent opposition. To cut a long story short, the connection between Cherie Blair and what our fathers/grandfathers said to our mothers/grandmothers leapt from the lead story of the *Independent on Sunday* last weekend.

That newspaper revealed that in her independent life as a barrister, where she works under her own name of Booth, Cherie B. had successfully prosecuted a poor man on welfare and got him clapped in Brixton Prison for not paying his poll tax. She was working on a series of such cases for various councils. He was getting income support of £44 a week and had about £4 left over after paying for food, electricity and rent. His poll tax arrears amounted to £200.62 and a previous offer to pay them off at £5 a week had been turned down. He described Cherie B. as 'ruthless'.

Put that side by side with the name 'Blair' in the headline and the distinctly unattractive three column picture of Ms Booth/Mrs Blair spread across one of the most readable British Sundays and you begin to make the connection. The picture shows a woman with protruding eyes. Her wide Julia Roberts(ish) mouth is gaping to reveal nearly all her teeth. (Vampires?)

The fact that the case took place late in 1993 when Tony Blair was still (to most people) just a pretty face and John Smith was alive and leader of the Labour Party is downplayed. It was also a time when Tony Blair sounded a bit like one of those made-up names pop stars like Cliff Richard invented. Or the sort of name that trendy hairdressers adopted. Cherie B. had not yet come into the picture. That she is a prominent barrister working in employment and public law and in a system where she takes cases in rotation is played down.

This story was redolent of the way the US media have been treating Hillary Rodham Clinton for several years. The consequences of muttering 'Yea', 'Cool' or 'OK' to the invitation to be buried with his people have always been immense for women. But they are usually well and truly shackled before they begin to find out the significance of the unread and unspoken fine print. This story also shows that no matter how times change, no matter how women succeed under their own steam, if they have the gall to show off their talents the upshot is that they are 'buried', if not with their husband's people then with his job and his identity. In modern times and in a visible job like politics, the former would be infinitely preferable to the latter.

There are several things about marriage I have never managed to fathom and having remained a spinster this far, I never want to find out. One of the few sensible observations about it I have read or heard over the years was made by Beatrice Webb – who with her husband Sidney was a Fabian and one of the outstanding social reformers of their time. Back in September 1918 while the couple were staying with Virginia and Leonard Woolf at Asheham Manor, their (rented) country house in Sussex, Beatrice off-loaded just some of her opinions on life to V. W., who documented them meticulously and with vicious pleasure in her diary. The doughty Beatrice had far too many opinions about every subject under the sun for V. W.'s liking. 'She proceeded to warn me against the dissipation of energy in emotional friendship. One should have only one great personal relationship in one's life, or at most two – marriage and parenthood. Marriage was necessary as a waste-pipe for emotion, as security in old age when personal attractiveness fails and as a help to work.' As she and V. W. plodded across the Sussex Downs, she added, 'Yes, I daresay an old family servant would do as well.'

Indubitably, Mrs Webb. Bring back the old family servant at once, I say, having never understood the rash compromise women can make on marriage, apparently effortlessly. I have never understood how women can give up their own names and take on new ones. In a random survey of *The Irish Times* newsroom, the overwhelming majority of the youngish men said they certainly could not imagine taking on the name of another at a time when they are roughly through one-third of their lives. Neither could they imagine shredding or diffusing their own identities to fit in with their wives/spouses/partners. Neither did they expect their wives to do it. But equally they have (mostly) never applied their minds to the business of which name the children should take or whose career is more important. A couple of the early twenties young men thought the whole thing was a bit of a joke for the elderly to bother about.

So how does the bitching about the super-wives come about? Who starts it? Who is to blame for the fallout? And is there a future for super-wives? Is there a need for them? More importantly, what do they get out of it? These are some of the questions that must be concentrating the mind of Chérie B. with the heat of her very own first real roasting from the media still sizzling around the backrooms and the ever-increasing number of drawing rooms of the British Labour Party. And this is even before she gets her foot in the door of Number 10.

One wonders how any intelligent woman looking across the Atlantic and seeing the public gutting of and attempts to humiliate HRC would even bother to put herself on the platform with an ambitious husband. It would seem that Chérie Blair has done it, apparently willingly. Without even moving from London or the hinterland of Westminster, she could have seen the awful treatment of Norma Major for the totally opposite reasons of refusing to become a party groupie and for refusing to be made over. What we do know is that, yet again, a woman is being used by the boys to brighten up boring party politics. The only modern thing about this case is that it has made the front page at a time when Tony Blair is facing splits in his own ranks, long before the next election is called. From this one can only deduce that a woman's role has become more important in doing her man down.

Just another backhand compliment. Back to the drawing board. Again.

26 January 1995

BOYS' GAMES

They never tire of promoting themselves and reinventing one another in more and more glamorous roles. Who do they think they're kidding?

Who would you say is more frazzled this week – John Major or me? I say it is me. Here's why. Mr M. has his Norm to keep him warm. He has a policeman outside the door to stop burglars, bully-boys from the North, Euro-sceptics and others who want to frame him. He has a big salary and other creature comforts, will go down in history and probably will go on attracting lovies for ever and ever. I have always considered him incredibly sexy and wondered why there is all the baffled incredulity about his frolics with women.

And me? Heading into my fourth International Women's Day (since covering Women's Affairs) and not one damn thing has changed. Each year the days leading up to 8 March have been fraught with anguish and grief. This year it looks like there will be no difference. On two out of the three previous years we ended up running a page at the last minute and I had to be dragged from the gas oven after each 'celebratory' event. Already this week I have been stalking the World Service at ungodly hours and doing the ironing at 4.30 GMT while following Marcel Pagnol's *Jean de Florette*.

Just back from Kerry this week with my stress levels

controlled by the gales and furiously angry seas, the angst has already set in. The whole business is particularly tiresome when the country is coming down yet again with menzone history, menzone celebrations. Not in any particular order, I am already alternately seething and yawning over two of these thingys that will fill the year with feverish, fervid and futile chat. Let no one try to con me that the word debate should be used to describe the rubbish that will be churned out.

One is another F-word – the Famine. The other is Michael Collins. The fact that the latter will be totally confused with Liam Neeson in the minds of most of the people on this island is neither here nor there for the boring academics, journalists, historians and all the usual pundits who come to something resembling life when they are dissecting 'our past'. It ain't my past, boys (and some girls). I have my own famine, still alive and thriving; more than enough to starve on. I may not be hungry for food – although at least one million on the island are – but I am ravenous for soul sustenance. I want the things that the Big Fellas, Long Fellas, Square Fellas and every other kind of fella (for foreigners, these soubriquets are the height of macho praise) swore they would give every 'citizen' when they got their way. Like being an equal. Like getting the same pay as male citizens. Like getting the same job chances. Like not being penalised for having a womb and having kids. And so on and on and on.

I found Irish history incredibly boring. A rising here. It flopped. A rising there. It flopped. In fact they never managed to get anything right. Like in the Abbey plays the women were always caoining and producing moonshine or tea for all shapes and sizes of fellas. I am not dismissive of the Famine. But I am extremely dubious about the welter of theories of its effect on our minds, our spirits, our present-day problems. A bit like Irish missionaries who go to save foreign countries so that they can escape taking on the rot eating into life at home.

It is impossible to dismiss the physical evidence which is all around us without ever going to Strokestown House. There is a Famine graveyard outside Listowel that I revisited last week. Yet again the eerie quiet and empty feel of the place left its mark. In the same week I was told about another graveyard in Ballybunion which has been built over. Obviously women were always involved – it is the writing out of their involvement that maddens me.

The real famines that happened in my lifetime are still stark and recent. There were the entire families that closed their doors and went to England. To us as children these things seemed to happen overnight. Nobody said they had been starving before they went. There was no palpable evidence of blight. They left behind houses that gradually fell into disrepair. Some returned. Of those many went away again. Most have never come back except perhaps for holidays. We met at Irish dances. Many married each other. Their children went to Irish and dancing classes every week. They won prizes, prizes without much value in other cultures.

So when the politicians in Leinster House start squabbling about how few votes they can get away with allocating to emigrants, I really throw up. I took the boat at eighteen like loads of others. My heart broke over and over. I hated this country. I loved it. The passion, the despair, the goddam emptiness getting the Limerick bus after a couple of weeks' holidays is the stuff that colours my vision of this country. When I saw the condescending politicians arriving in Irish clubs and centres to dispense token plamás in London and other places on St Patrick's Day, I got so angry. That's famine for you. There is not much difference between dying of starvation in your own patch and being pitched overboard.

What is all this fuss about Michael Collins? He was born, lived, killed and was killed. All in the name of what? Because Dev lived, we know that he was a cold calculating and complex man who was so terrified of women, or disliked them or hated them so much, that he deliberately ensured they would forever put up and shut up. I saw him once. I saw just another old man in a dark coat. So? The two of them are long dead. Alive, according to menzone lore, Collins was a great fella altogether. Fit and flirty and fierce handsome. He could lure the birds from the trees and seduce high-born ladies. And there was a native who won his heart, Kitty something? – at least that's what Neil Jordan said recently. No doubt some famous beauty will be found to flesh out that bit, to add colour and bump up the takings at the box office. Like everything else about this knackered little island you can take it as read that each and every decision about Collins and company will be taken outside the country. London yesterday, Washington, Brussels and Tokyo today. LA tomorrow.

The main point is that Collins could not do what he

was supposed to do. From vague bits out of boring menzone Irish history I seem to remember that he was hopelessly outmanoeuvred by the British. The way I see it is pretty simple. The man was no damn good at his job. I have always believed in not believing what I was told by men. If Collins could not do it he should have handed it over to someone else, but they were all a pretty wimpish lot anyway. B-o-r-ing.

Consign Collins et al to the bin of history and consider the present. Are the current Collinses and would-be Devs going to make this country any different for women? The bottom line is, what's in it for me? Has any woman dotted a 't' in this famous Framework Document? Were they just around to make the tea, to take the bare look off the men? To try to convince us that men are changing, writing a new agenda, building a frame with equal compartments? That is the way I will be looking at the F-document. In my mind there are just two kinds of people – men and women, regardless of race, creed, age or colour. The men do. The women do as they are told.

So watch all the words as well as the F ones. Read them well. If you do not, if you let them away with anything, as sure as night follows day the eventual agreement about this petty little island will exclude you as much as it has done in the past. Like the women textile workers in the US who fought and died in their own famines to put women's bums on (a few) boardroom chairs. It was their struggle that created International Women's Day. And who cares? I do. Sympathy cards for its demise in this neck of the woods will be greatly appreciated.

23 February 1995

NOW MY CHILD HAS FLOWN

Mothers and fathers loved this and could see the parallels with their own lives.

Sometimes I think I miss Friday evenings most. I would pick her up at school. If I was late she would lunge at the car and say, 'I thought you were never coming.' She would throw her eyes up to heaven to her few pals to indicate what an oddball of a mother she had. If I was early, I would sit in the car and listen to the play, or whatever, on Radio 4. One year I heard *The Forsyte Saga* again almost in its entirety. For several years it had the books' programme at that time.

We would go to McDonald's for burgers and coke. She hated the bit of gherkin. I loved it and got hers as well as mine. Usually I had done the shopping and it was in the boot of the car. If it had been a demented week the boot would be empty. She would grab the list and fly around the supermarket, getting only what we needed and bringing back change. I always bought more than I intended and came out broke. We would shop for a treat – a pretty box, a special card, another soft toy with a name like Sloopy to add to the collection. In the early days, she would get the comic she was into at the time. But for years it has been *Hello!* She has always had a reverential attitude to magazines and books, hating it if you flicked through the pages, putting a hint of a crease or a thumb-mark on the unread pages. Then it was home to light the fire, pull the curtains on the world and settle down to the *Late Late Show* and *Hello!* with a bowl of pasta on our knees. Until we got home there would be bursts of conversation about the dramas of the week; fits and starts of chat which could not wait. Later in the evening it would start all over again, in more detail, when adjustment had set in.

Those days are gone. Last Friday my daughter was twenty-one. In fact, they have been gone for some time and I have been stealthily buying *Hello!* anyway. But it was only the watershed of twenty-one that wrenched long-forgotten memories out of the quicksand last week, that threw me into a wallow of *déjà vu.*

It was Friday evening. I was pulling the curtains with *Hello!* in my hand. The shopping was dumped unpacked on the floor when I suddenly felt a burst of emptiness. It was a few seconds before I realised that the missing factor was herself. She should have been tut-tutting about who had been in her room and who had moved one of her china animals or other ornaments the tiniest iota left or right. She should have been asking if it was time to ring Nana or if there was any post. Or about the Arrangements for the weekend. In our lives and those of our friends, her obsession with what was happening when, where and at what exact time assumed the proportion of capital letters as she grew up. It became a jokey thing, especially when she passed it on to Jack, her surrogate young brother who was twelve last week, the day after she was twenty-one.

Almost from the day he came home from hospital, she assumed a proprietorial claim on Jack. He was the first baby of our neighbours, Peter and Margaret. She fed him, changed him, played with him and pushed him around in a pram or anything on wheels she could find. Her pride in him was immense. Any new move he made, any hint of a change was noted. By the time he was two, she had declared him a genius – a view she still holds. Quite right too. She would drag him into town, trail the reluctant child around the shops and take him to places she wanted to visit herself by bribing him with ice-cream and Dinky cars.

Because of my erratic working life, she went to boarding school at the age of eight. It was a calculated risk and it worked. I will never forget the first Friday afternoon when I arrived on time at Aravon to pick her up. She was almost down at the gate, her blazer dragging along behind her, looking anxiously at each car as it went by. I nearly passed out but she jumped in and immediately started waving to her new friends. She swears she cannot remember my vision of it. Sometimes she tries to blackmail me by threatening to write a *Mommy Dearest* kind of book.

We wrote letters each week. They usually crossed in the post but it did not matter. It happened by accident because we both like writing letters. Years later I realised how long some weeks can be, the ones when you seem to have covered a lifetime by Friday – good, bad and indifferent. By the time she went to Rathdown, she was well up on boarding-school life: sewing on the name tags, getting in the queue for the swapped uniforms and other things that I had always been hopeless at.

I will not go on too much about her. Without realising it, I need a sharp kick to stop sounding like the mother of the bride. What I do know is that without the shape, the routine she has put on my life for many years, I am now flailing around in the fashion of ships without rudders or planes without wings. Even though she is still living at home, our lives run in opposite directions. Sometimes days pass without our seeing each other. We leave notes. 'We are out of . . . milk, what cereal? bread, fusilli, loo paper.' Things like that.

I have spent the last week wallowing in the nostalgia of the Sunday afternoon trips to Powerscourt or the Zoo, or brisk walks down and up Dun Laoghaire pier with friends and their children. I know they were all often fighting, crying or throwing up at the same time but I remember only the sugary sweetness of it. If it rained, it was only a fleeting shower. It was never freezing; just crisp and sunny. Every mid-term break and holiday we went to Kerry. She usually spent entire summers down there so that my own mother became another mother figure. She was the one who asked: 'When were you at Confession last?' She nearly passed out when my daughter started adding on the piece of the 'Our Father' that Protestants say. I think she had grave reservations about how I was having her educated but like the nice woman she is, let it pass. Or made a novena.

So she is twenty-one and I have realised I cannot go on saying I am still thirty-nine. She is full of purpose. She will travel the world. She will conquer LA. She will discover lost tribes. What about me?

I have run out of excuses for not doing all the things I swore I wanted to do. If I, who have always kept the day job going, feel as blank, empty and destitute as a new piece of blotting paper now that my child has flown, what do women feel who have dedicated their entire lives to them? Much the same, I imagine. It is only now that I sleep lightly until she is in at night that I realise why my own mother still worries when I am not home at a reasonable time. After all these years she has not got used to the fact that I just forget the time. That the hours fly by.

This story has two endings:

1   Oh Lord, thou art hard on mothers.
2   I love you, babe.

9 March 1995

Cinema as a Portrayal of Life

It is undeniable that film, more than any other art form, has kept a vigilant eye on the changes in our lives. They may be faulted for glamorising issues, but they are streets ahead of books and paintings.

Coming out of the Stella Cinema in Rathmines, the other evening, I gratefully lit up a fag and took lungfuls of carbon monoxide. You would need a dose of your favourite poison after the rubbish I had just seen.

'Coffin nail,' muttered a little, but not young, male worm as he slithered past me on his way in to the next showing of *Disclosure*. Watching him as he scuttled towards the door, I knew damn well this was an individual with attitude. He gave a quick look over his shoulder to see what the reaction was. He had late-night heavy breather/early-morning flasher written all over the back of him. Greasy hair, a stringy scarf that did not hide a burgeoning boil on his neck and greying denims that did not disguise his spindly, bandy legs. I suspect he came out of *Disclosure* with a sloppy grin on his chops. He is the sort of fan I would expect Michael Douglas to have when he is playing the issue movies where women are distorted yet again. They are not strong. They are raving lunatics. The man, aka Douglas, is the poor headless chicken who is driven demented when these women pursue him (almost) to the death. For sex,

sex and more sex.

The films – *Fatal Attraction, Basic Instinct, Disclosure* – should actually be named something like *Stand by Your Man* 1 and 2 and 3. They make a fortune at the box office and are as sickening as the Doris Day films of the 1950s. The ones where she was fantastically pretty and talented and hid it under her apron while propping up her husband and his career. The plot consisted of a panic when DD realised she had potential for something apart from smiling sweetly and making her own tomato ketchup. She was tempted to behave like a real person with her own bank account but was lured back by the manipulative tantrums of her man.

The only significance of these movies – and film has tended to be much better at logging social history than other media – is that they reflect the issues of the day. In *Disclosure*, Douglas is portraying one of that much-vaunted, apparently endangered American species – the white, middle-class, middle-aged man. Demi Moore, the coldly hysterical hussy, is portraying all the women in the world who want to get a chance at a top job.

That man, the story goes, is doing all the right things. He works his ass off to provide a life of sweetness and light for a wife and two kids. They live in a smashing pad, look and behave like WASPs. The wives are always cool, shining-clean and glamorous in an elegant way. Kids are pretty and precocious. You would grind your teeth with envy at the places they live in. In *Disclosure*, the house in the pretty suburbs outside Seattle is a combination of an English country cottage (mansion to me) outside – all ivy and roses and flagged paths – and Temple Bar apartment; acres of light-filled space you would never want to leave. Then along comes some deadly Other Woman who throws the perfect jigsaw up in the air, and you've got a movie.

I have not seen *Basic Instinct* but the other two are enough to give you the drift. However, *Disclosure* is a con in more ways than one. Briefly, Douglas plays a man in a computer corporation. He is waiting to be promoted. At the last minute, a woman is brought in over his head. The head of the company makes a pretty speech about breaking glass ceilings and the like.

Played by Demi Moore, the Wicked Witch looks as if she could shoot through any roof she cared for, bypassing ceilings of concrete, let alone glass. Moore does not just want Michael's job. She wants him. So she invites him to sample some pretty rare wine and starts throwing herself – literally – at him. It all happens in her office so she is flinging herself and him over noisy equipment with a lot of noisy moaning. Were they plants that tumbled down? Douglas is half-hooked about half-way through. Then he sees the light and pulls up his trousers and races home to shower off the memory. There are four nasty scratches on his chest. As sex scenes go it is brilliantly awful.

The next morning she reports him for sexual harassment. It is then you realise you are being totally conned. I don't want to give away the whole thing, but you realise that the turnabout 'sexual harassment is about power' message trotted out by the publicists has only a smidgin to do with the real story. I gather Michael Crichton's book, on which it is based, is a walloping good read. The film is the pits. For me, there are only a couple of points worth making about *Fatal Attraction* and *Disclosure*. The guys always win. Their beautiful and intelligent wives stick by them despite their goings-on. In *FA*, the real point was lost under the welter of Glenn Close's mania. She, a fast lady on the loose, slept with him while his wife was out of town. She took it seriously as women are inclined to do. He did not. He expected her to have his own one-night-stand-and-see-you-around attitude. In *Disclosure*, Demi Moore cooks her own goose when she goes into a passionate rant about being a woman, being expected to dress up like a woman and do a man's job according to their squalid values.

What is also important about these films is that they show the huge and growing fissure, with its consequent nastiness, that exists between men and women. And there are other features of what could be described as sexual harassment not yet spoken about. For example, a few weeks ago in the middle of the newsroom, colleague Pat Langan was telling me a story. He threw an arm over my shoulders. A second later his face seized up with blind panic and he jumped backwards. A further second, his face went into relief. 'Thank God it's only you,' he said. (If you hang around here long enough you're sure to get a compliment for something.) The problem is, he said seriously, that there are now very few women with whom men feel comfortable enough to give them the odd affectionate hug, tell them they're looking good or crack a risqué joke in their presence.

The lovely lady in the office around the corner in College Green says, with more than a grain of nostalgia, that she misses the banter. 'It made me feel good. It did make me feel attractive. Things were different then.' And there is another terrific colleague who is a grandfather. He loves kids and used to take his neighbour's two to the park and buy them sweets. 'I stopped it and I told her why.' His neighbour agreed with him that in the current climate his actions would be seen as, at best, doubtful and at worst, probably worth reporting.

The answer? I guess we can't have it all.

16 March 1995

THE FIRST GABRIEL

To my shame I had a whopper of a mistake in the original piece, accusing Gay Byrne of asking the new women TDs who was at home minding their children while they appeared on the Late Late Show. *In fact he had simply conveyed the query of a viewer. I apologised and got the most generous and warm reply. I am saving it to frame for my grandchildren.*

Is Gay Byrne sexy? What makes him successful with women? Why do they mob him outside RTE and block the lines to his radio programme every morning? Why do they open their souls and tell him their most intimate secrets? Secrets they have not told friends, priests or psychiatrists? Why do they flirt with him? Why do they rebuke him playfully for saying he prefers Princess Di or Meryl Streep to any woman in the world?

Is his a cerebral appeal? Is he a safe fantasy? Does he evoke the name of his wife, Kathleen Watkins, just often enough to let his fans know he is spoken for?

Watching the Calor Gas Housewife of the Year show on Monday night you could only wonder at the extent of his charm over the six finalists. These were no bimbos. The woman who won – Philomena Delaney from Limerick – was a walking, talking advertisement for Superwoman of the Year. The Calor Housewife competition is a sort of Rose of Tralee for mammies. It is the fifteen minutes of fame for six women who are similar to many others in homes all over the country doing amazing work for no pay and little visible acclaim. (Since the word 'housewife' and phrases like 'I'm only a housewife' are rapidly disappearing from the vocabulary, I am told by a spokeswoman for the organisers that they will be reconsidering the title of this event.)

Philomena Delaney, bright and beautiful, was certainly no 'only' anything. You could only wonder how there are enough hours in the day for the amount of work she does – apart from part-time paid work, she is involved in numerous voluntary activities in her community, from helping the handicapped to working with a women's project in Southill. She bakes for the fun of it. Boy, oh boy, as my father used to say. Like the others, she had cooked an amazing meal – fettucine al something and something else that sounded colourful for desert.

All six finalists were confident and assured. And they survived as women in their own right in spite of things like the awful tips they were invited to pass on to other wives of houses. One told you to stick a skewer or something through potatoes and they would bake quicker. I think even I knew that. Another suggested putting scrunched-up tin foil on a pastry base to avoid 'a soggy bottom'. Apart from the women's self-possession, what was also forcefully obvious was the open way they responded to Gaybo. You could feel the chemistry. Even the more serious of them were a little artless, a bit arch, a touch roguish with Mr Byrne. Only you could never imagine them using this title. To them and to hosts of other women, he is simply 'Gay'.

As everyone knows, the whole political correctness thing has totally bypassed Gay Byrne. He still asks women (usually the first question) what their husbands do. Then he asks how many children they have. So immediately he is compounding the old habit of defining over half the population in terms of the jobs their husbands have. Or how many children they have. And how successful the children are. And so on.

That does not seem to faze his constituency of women listeners and watchers. It can hardly be that the world has entirely passed him by, but I have not yet heard anyone pick him up or chastise him on it. This is 1995. They are not all Cork mammies who are still saying, 'Help, help, my son the engineer is drowning.' Most women of this class and self-image nowadays would be more likely to say, 'Help, help, I'm an engineer but I can't swim and . . . '

Maybe it does not matter. Maybe he is asking the questions that we all want answered anyway but in these days of caution and rules, are afraid to ask. For myself, it is something that would not usually cross my mind when I first meet a woman or a man. What a woman's husband/man's wife does during the day is usually irrelevant – unless she/he is unemployed or loaded.

Agewise, many of his women listeners are much younger than him. So the age thing does not seem to matter. Philomena Delaney, for example, would hardly have been out of rompers when GB became a star on television. She would have been in school when his radio programme started. Others, who are older, have remained faithful to him. Over the years I have seen his attitude towards women change – on television. On radio it is still much the same. But on the box, up to about five, six or seven years ago, he appeared distinctly uncomfortable with strong/articulate/challenging women. He would purse his lips a bit like a parish priest confronted with a reserved sin. He would talk down to them. He would use his expertise – it seemed to me – to push them into a corner, to dismiss them or to trivialise their arguments. With women who were coy, flirtatious or unsure, he was beaming and benevolent, putting them at their ease, calming them down or playing up to them.

The change came imperceptibly and was so subtle that it was a bit of a chicken-and-egg thing. Either Gay Byrne grew accustomed to confident women as he grew older or the number of women of this kind has grown. But there are still inconsistencies. And even though it is 1995 and the clergy are filling up pages of newsprint with the evidence of their own problems, Gay Byrne still sticks to the old-fashioned formula of showing his respect for and chumminess with priests and other such by calling them 'Father Jo' or 'Bishop Joachim' or whatever. It was the way that people who had a priest in the family addressed them – when it was a real bonus to be able to claim one as a relative.

I suspect that Gay Byrne's instinctive approach, the language he uses and the way he treats people are part of his consummate skill as a broadcaster and the reason why he remains so popular. I doubt if his tactics are thought out much in advance. What you see is what he feels. It is spontaneous. And what he feels is still a fair barometer of how most Irish men (and women) believe that ambitious women and the clergy should be handled. Take ambitious women, for example: by making them jump through hoops, he and the country are making them realise who is still in control.

But getting back to starters, is Gay Byrne sexy? The only answer is a hollering 'yes'. You can see it in the way women respond to him – their body language as they seek to please him, or just seek a reaction. And let's face it, it's all (mostly) good, clean fun. It makes you feel better when you see one Rose handing her tiara over to her happy and tearful successor or the 1994 Housewife draping the 1995 sash on the winner. And in the background, there is GB radiating happiness. A few stray tears wandered down my cheeks the other night. God, I must be going soft.

6 April 1995

OF MEN AND WHAT THEY DO TO US

I got a lot of personal mail from women in the last year, and an increasing amount from men. Men's initial assumption is that I hate them in a sweeping, generalised way. Not true. But many are only beginning to cotton on to the truth – life as defined by men suits no human being.

'Why do you hate men?' This was the first question on a prepared list from a young fella who came to interview me recently. He is a student at one of the many schools of journalism/communications/media studies. He looked about nineteen. They were going to be in charge of a radio station for a week and were preparing bits and pieces for this and that.

'Hate? Wha'?' Talk about taking the wind out of your sails and loosening your false teeth. I froze. Was he right? Was it a case of truth or whatever coming out of the mouths of babes? To cover my confusion, I swallowed a fag, ate a packet of mints, took a fit of bronchial coughing, drank a litre of mineral water, went to the women's room, put more kohl around my eyes, waxed my hair and came back trying to look my age to interface with the little innocent relentlessly waiting with his mike poised.

'I do not hate men.' The growl came through clenched teeth. Then, with a bit more gravitas and poise as befitting my senior years, I told him slowly and carefully that it was not men I hated but the society they had developed. What I hate is the man-made world I am forced to live in. It is the fact that women are ruthlessly exploited in this double-standard orb, that men define my life (or try their damnedest), that they make wars and beat up women. That men are deemed successful if they simply accumulate money and power in the marketplace while they ignore the kids they have fathered until they get old and lonely and realise that gold cards and bimbos ain't everything. That men get more take-home pay than women doing the same jobs. That they get bigger helpings in restaurants. At home they get the steak while their wives pretend they are dieting. That their women have to sleep with them if they want a new mink or vacuum cleaner or something. That most young men confidently expect to be a woman's boss (even an older woman's boss) in a few years' time. That he – or any of the clones that look/sound/think like him – might be useless at that and many jobs is irrelevant in the world that men have made. But they get these kind of 'When I rule the world' notions from the special and rigid Bible for Men which is passed on in the secret, coded language of this male-ist life.

They get it from brothers, fathers, teachers, judges, politicians and the rest of the M-gang who set the standards in this world – a universe, incidentally, that, for all their smartness, they cannot run, cannot feed and about which they have a plug-the-nearest-gap, Sellotape-it-over set of answers for its problems.

The Bible of Women – also written by men – is vague, complex, designed to confuse and full of shit about love.

This is the answer to everything in a woman's life. You are seen to be successful if you can get and keep the love of any old tyke. You are seen to be successful if the old ass has piles of lolly. Forget about his wobbly chins and other turn-offs. M. M. got it right, baby, you are told. Diamonds are a gal's best friend. That is all very well if you look like M. M. on the outside, are miserable inside and end up getting blown away by some mafia or other because you picked the wrong man in the wrong place at the wrong time. Or something. It's all male-written history anyway. Who believes anything they write?

This outpouring is caused by thinking of Ailbhe Smyth and the helluva do she is planning for next weekend – from the evening of Friday nineteenth, through Saturday twentieth, and, by the sounds of it, well into Sunday. Smyth, the director of the Women's Studies Department in UCD (Women's Resource and Research Centre – WERRC), is inviting everyone to go along and celebrate the twenty-fifth anniversary of the Irish Women's Liberation Movement. There will be the founders of that movement and those who have tagged along over the years. There will be the new kids trying to reshape the block.

According to the literature, there will be any amount of discussions on every subject going related to women, from sisterhood to lesbians, economic issues, citizenship, violence and sexual exploitation, racism and much more including She-Bop – feminism, rock, pop and rap.

I will be out of the country that weekend. I was also away when the Women's Liberation Movement started here, I was not on the condom train or involved in anything much that went on here for a heady three years or so. However, the Angry Fairy must have given me an extra lash of the wand because I have been steaming with rage ever since I found out that there is one agenda for men and a totally different destiny set out for women.

In recent days we have seen one of the most blatantly extravagant commemorations of a war in which men hacked each other to death, bombed, maimed and disfigured each other, raped and plundered. Some cried and held their comrades while they died. Others went mad. And so on. But this week, apart from the solemn tones, the whole thing has been more like a celebration. Armies of men in grey suits and uniforms. Where have women figured? They were most splendidly encapsulated in the pictures and headlines showing the Queen Mother, one of those who came shining radiantly through but shedding a few gentle, feminine tears into a hankie. God's in his heaven. And so on and so on.

A few flying hours away from the balcony of Buckingham Palace, there is a brutal war still going on among Serbs, Croats and Bosnians. Another in Rwanda. Another in Afghanistan. Nuclear plants spew diseases into the atmosphere. The effects of the atom bomb are still producing deformed children, cancers and other tragedies. 'Oklahoma' will never be sung about with gusto again. And more, more, more. So what has been achieved by women in the last twenty-five years? You could say a lot when you consider that women had sweet damn all. Giving up jobs on marriage. No women on juries. No woman could get things on hire purchase without their husband's signature. In short, a right old mess.

But what have we today? Not much. What I would do about immediate issues is:

1   Unemployment: mandatory jobsharing from the top down.
2   Criminalise private and public sector employers who do not bring in a fifty/fifty job ratio within six months. Implement with massive fines and prison sentences. Ditto the trade unions.
3   Violence against women; put the men in refuges, leave the women and kids at home.
4   Divorce: women should not get married. It is a service to suit men. If they must, it should be copperfastened with a pre-nuptial agreement down to the last crossed 't' from big issues to the minutiae about who does the ironing – it is things like this that cause separations. Everything should be renegotiated regularly.
5   Abortion: Leave the whole issue to women.
6   One of the most important groups of women whose cause was not addressed twenty-five years ago were those who bring up their families, run houses and such for no pay. There has been a bitter division between these women and those they call 'careerists'. This feud must be made up. Women's experience raising children should be an acceptable part of their CVs if they want to go back to work.
7   Many more successful women must open up and support others of their own sex. They must give

up the Queen Bee thing and actively promote other women for jobs. Women politicians and those in other job areas with unsocial hours should stop hiding their families. They must tell the world what it is like to do a heavy day's work and come home to tired children/husband and spend their weekends scrubbing, cleaning and shopping.

Women TDs and senators should be demanding a nine-to-five day. They should look at the ponderous, time-consuming way legislation is dealt with. Talk about all the unnecessary time wasted. They must actively seek quotas or targets and positive discrimination. And more.

Finally, one thing that I've always been too timid to ask. Why did they bring back condoms twenty-five years ago? If it was symbolic then, OK. But it is time the tokenism was dropped. Make the boys grow up. After twenty-five years of silence by too many women, it is time we opened up and told the story as it is. Forget about reports, reviews, commissions. Shame the men with the truth.

11 May 1995

FEAR OF THE F-WORD

Unfortunately, most successful women seem to have lost touch with the philosophy of feminism. It has become a dirty word. Some are closet feminists. Do they realise that without its driving force they might as well stay at home and take the pocket money?

Get wise. Take an eye-bath and slough off the rose-tinted scales. Before wasting any more energy, stop, take stock, unravel the pseudo-babble. Forget about equality. It will never happen, baby. Not for you and (barring an act of some she-god) not for your daughters. After that, who cares? We will all be six foot under or floating round the heavens – in the pink zone.

If any of you out there are still hopeful, close your eyes now and pass by. The reason? This is a deeply pessimistic but passionately realistic view of the world for women. If any of you feel you are still fighting the revolution, forget it. Roll up the banners. Burn the barricades. If you want to carry on pretending, just buy a new power suit and carry on copying the boys. Or flirt for a powerful man and live in his space for as long as he lets you. Forget about idiotic symbols – things like getting 'obey' taken out of the marriage service and calling yourself 'Ms'. Singly or together, Miss, Mrs and Ms all add up to zilch. Regardless of what handle you choose, your place is still in the holding queue. If you think this is just light-hearted prattle, it is not. Neither is it idle and gloomy despair. It is born out of covering the reality of women's lives – still quaintly called Women's Affairs – for five years.

Half-way through 1995, I look back at the foolish and innocent dreams, hopes and ideals I started off with five years ago. The belief that women were finally on the brink of a major breakthrough, that they would be allowed to behave like adults, that they could be taken seriously, was honestly held. All around me I could see countless women poised to take control in any number of jobs, in all areas of power. These were no loonies from the left, right or centre. They were intelligent, educated and opinionated – many of them being helped by supportive spouses. Some held the political views of the traditional, mainstream, male-run parties but their party politics played second fiddle to the politics of women's lives. Almost to a woman, among themselves, they spoke the same shorthand language shared by women from all cultures and backgrounds.

I was codded by the belief that while men might still be reluctant to give up the power, it would be gently eased from them by the demographics of the new Ireland in the new Europe. 'Look at the figures,' I was told. Those figures showed rapidly shrinking families which were producing as many skilled girls as boys. The theory was that at the very least it would be enormously wasteful for countries to tie women to the kitchen sinks when so much of national budgets had been invested in their education. If all else failed, the brute forces of the marketplace would win through. And there was more, much more buoyancy and expectancy. God, my spectacles must have been real pinko shades.

What has really happened is worse than sweet damn all. If it was only SDA, we could still rage and holler, march, make tracks to the European Court, embarrass the suits in power. The worst conquest of all is that a minimalist, eeny-meeny number of women have won through, just enough to take the spare look off the suit photocalls.

With that has come the appalling vista that feminists down through the years have always feared and railed against. The women who pushed their way through have simply taken male agendas. Gone are the Utopian dreams of a brave new world with female values emerging to create new and civilising standards. I will not even mention the stopping of wars or the crushing of the weak still further underfoot. Not even through the rosiest of specs had I gone that far. I would have been happy, in the relative short-term, with a target date of the year 2000 for equal numbers in politics, the power structures of various churches, the judiciary, civil service and so on. I would have been content if having and rearing children carried a major plus on a woman's CV. I would have been happy to have quotas in every forum, including the Oireachtas, for elderly people, for under-twenty-fives, for disabled people. And so on.

So what have we got? What would an alien from space landing here for the first time see? First, she would hear a woman's voice only occasionally and hardly ever with tones of authority. She could listen to RTE radio for about eight hours from early morning to afternoon without hearing a woman – except for the snatches where one reads the news. She could read the newspapers and see women shown in a trivial or inferior way. They would usually be young and smiling or crying.

Take politics as an example of an area where women have made huge gains in less than five years. What is the difference between them and their male colleagues? With Mildred Fox raising the number of women TDs to twenty-two, and the Seanad eight bringing the Oireachtas total to the big thirty, questions beg to be asked. Is there any difference in voting for a woman? What changes have they made to the medieval, expensive and time-consuming way of doing their business?

The short answer is none. The whole carry-on is hostile to deputies and senators, not to mention the voters, and by now, three years after the great leap forward in 1992, there has not been a mutter of dissent from the elected women. Several years ago I heard Harriet Harman of the British Labour Party, describe in devastating detail how the parliamentary system had evolved and still had not changed. It was, she said, a set-up devised to suit the squires, merchants et al, who slotted it in at the end of a real day's work. They would ramble in around dinnertime and happily prattle on through the night.

Though the membership has changed somewhat, the system is still much the same. Why are not women politicians (most of whom have young children) calling for a nine-to-five day and a four-day week? Why are they not calling the men's bluff and spelling out the facts about constituency work? Why not set up a series of public education clinics run by ordinary workers instead?

That might be all too simple. And it might rock boats. Holy cow, it might mean they would not get a nomination next time out. I will not even go into that rubbish that the Catholic Church is up to in its navel-gazing about married priests' jobs. There are thousands of other reasons for being extremely pessimistic if you are a woman. A colleague says that Michael Noonan is doing wonders for women's health – screening, counselling and oodles of goodies. They always existed for women with money. He still frowns worriedly about the reasons women go to England for abortions. If there was a woman in his job, she would not need to ask.

And then of course there's the UN women's conference at Beijing coming up. It will take many, many Beijings to get a glimmer of balance. *C'est la vie.*

6 July 1995

THE DIVORCE CAMPAIGN

Nora Bennis was one of the main players against divorce.
This was the first time I had a proper conversation with her.

So who is Nora Bennis anyway? Where does she come from? What is her agenda? What gives her the almighty right to tell the nation it will fall asunder if it gives divorce the thumbs-up on 24 November? That if you say you want to have another go at marriage, raise a second lot of children, you will be fast-forwarding the dawn of a Sodom and Gomorrah on the Island of Saints and Scholars?

'Nora Bennis is a zealot, isn't she? She simply entertains no doubts about anything. She is rigidly single-minded about what she believes in. Ian Paisley is a zealot. I cannot relate to people like them.' This is the view of one colleague.

Being described as a zealot would not faze Mrs B. More likely, the comment would draw a wry smile. She has been described as everything from a fanatic to a reactionary – and more. Last weekend, as she recited the litany of invective which has rained down on her, she sat upright on the sofa in the spacious lobby of the Limerick Ryan Hotel near her home and gave one of her saintly smiles. That is the only way to describe them. Her mouth curves in a sweet, generous arc. Not a hint of bitterness, sarcasm or cynicism; even a bit roguish at times. The funny thing is, she says, that most people – particularly her critics – form opinions about her before they have ever met her.

119

Nora Bennis has a sense of humour. She is neatly dressed in classic and dateless navy and white. She listens to questions and answers carefully and thoughtfully, never raising her voice to make or refute a point. Nora Bennis has shot to national fame in less than five years for her trenchant views on 'traditional values'. She was founder of 'Women Working at Home' in 1993 and is leader of the Solidarity Movement (July 1994), which intends running independent candidates in various elections. She was regarded as little more than a nuisance by the establishment parties until the European elections last year when her considerable success as an Independent in Munster quickly wiped the condescending smiles off their faces. She pulled in 18,424 first-preference votes, ending with a total of 24,982 when she was eliminated after the eighth count. Votes are the currency that politicians understand. They got the message. They will never underestimate Mrs Bennis again. They live in fear of the next general election and the challenges posed by Mrs Bennis.

'Most people in Solidarity are raw beginners like me. I think this is good. They are reacting to the failure of the political party system – and it is clear that system is failing, is losing control and is leaving more people with a feeling of helplessness and hopelessness.'

She is vigorously anti-abortion and sketches a doomsday scenario for this country if divorce is allowed. She is working flat-out to prevent its introduction and is a regular on local radio stations as well as national television and radio. Briefly, she believes that the 'liberal agenda' is now so pervasive a force in Ireland that it is the absolute

120

arbiter of the values we live by. The purveyors of this agenda have created a climate where all absolute principles of right and wrong have gone for a burton, leaving us in a climate where everybody from children up – she is particularly worried about the effects on children – feel free to form their own opinions on major moral issues such as abortion, euthanasia and divorce. She feels that Irish society is crippled and confused by the burden of living in a vacuum where absolutes no longer exist. She feels that, if introduced, divorce will hasten the decline in morality.

'The growing culture is one where people are encouraged to believe what they like. The result is that they say, "Well, I wouldn't do it (abortion/divorce) myself but if anybody else wants to, then I wouldn't oppose them." But surely the extension of that is you could say that if Hitler felt what he did was right, it was OK for him? I think, as a result, young people are being given a crazy sense of morality.'

Despite her strong reservations about political parties now, Nora Bennis was born into a strong nationalist and Fianna Fáil family. She is third in a family of five – two other children died at birth. Her father, Paul Shinners, was involved as a scout in the 1916 Rising and was imprisoned in the Curragh for thirty days. There he went on hunger strike. There is a note of pride when she says this. Her parents met in England where they had emigrated to find work and came back to Limerick in 1940, the year she was born, after the start of the Second World War. They lived in a corporation housing estate. Her father never had a permanent job. 'Materially, we were very much on the poverty line but in every other way we were very well off.'

Both he and her mother, Margaret, struggled to make ends meet but had high expectations for their children. Both, she says, were self-educated, and her mother, like most others at the time, made clothes for the children as well as running a home on very little. Nora went to the Presentation Convent but left early to go to the 'tech'. There she did a commercial course which helped her get a job as a clerk typist in Limerick Corporation.

Politics were an endless source of discussion in the house and Fianna Fáil was the tops. 'Anybody coming into our house would probably think that Dev was the real god because I think his picture was a bit bigger than the one of the Sacred Heart.' Her father's lifelong devotion to the Chief makes a poignant vignette. When Éamon de Valera died in August 1975 her father set off for Dublin to pay his respects at the lying-in-state. There was an unofficial boarding stage for the Dublin train when it slowed down outside Limerick. It meant climbing a steep embankment to get on and in the effort, Mr Shinners had a massive heart attack and died.

Nora Shinners met her husband, Gerry Bennis, while still in her teens. They went out for three or four years and were married when she was twenty-two. He works for Telecom but the GAA is his abiding passion. He and his brothers played for the county and he was chairman of the Limerick GAA county board for several years. They have four children aged between sixteen and thirty. Two of the three girls are teachers and the boy is a bricklayer in England. For Nora Bennis, her life of campaigning began a mere five years ago when she went to a conference on the family in Brighton – largely because Mother Teresa was expected to attend. Mother Teresa did not but Princess Di did. There, Mrs Bennis heard a cosmopolitan group of speakers of all religions speaking about the collapse of society in Britain and the United States as a result of the influence of the liberal agenda. When she came back to Ireland she looked around her and found that much of the 'damage' she had heard about in Brighton was already taking place here. After the 'X' case, she and some of her neighbours set up 'Mothers Working at Home' because of their feeling of isolation from what they believed in.

After four hours of solid listening, talking and arguing, I left Nora Bennis with much to think about. I disagree with many of her conclusions about Irish society and the reasons for the massive changes that have happened in a generation or so. I think she is too quick to see conspiracies behind these changes. I think she is too quick to dismiss women whom she disagrees with as 'the feminists' who have some sinister agenda of their own. I think she is pushing an uphill argument in trying to stop the tide of change, in wanting the return of Dev's Ireland. I could go on. What I do know is that I like Nora Bennis. And in the middle of much of what she is saying I heard echoes of the bewilderment, the confusion and the worries about bringing in divorce that I had listened to in the previous two weeks from a wide cross-section of people in Kerry.

She believes the referendum will be resoundingly defeated. Will she be proved right?

21 September 1995

C. J. H. AT SEVENTY

The charm and sexiness of the man never wanes. Neither does public interest in him – if my overwhelmingly positive mail is anything to go by.

There are real men. And there are *real* men. There are many men a woman might like/love/covet one day and forget the next. But there are the rare few men you want to be near, that you want to listen to, with whom you want to go on long journeys. They are the singular few you will remember with *tendresse* all your days. Well, at least a month. Or a week? But there are damn few who can make your heart flutter at 11.30 in the morning so that you float along on cloud nine all day.

Such a man is Charles J. Haughey. Even though the meeting was brief yesterday, the karma lingers on. The man who was seventy last Saturday was hosting a tea morning in aid of the Alzheimer's Society of Ireland on the front lawn of his home in Kinsealy. Abbeville and its grounds were superb in one of the most perfect September mornings. Barry's, who sponsored the tea, could never hope to get a blend as perfect, a mixture so addictive, as the man who served it. He was giving his support to the society because a good friend of his got the disease many years ago when it was not properly recognised.

They used to call him 'The Boss'. And many other things. All the adjectives and descriptions simply added to the charisma that made him loved and feared and created universal curiosity about him and his life. Followers and others tried to show off their smartaleckry by deriding him. Many of them are still around: still dull as ditchwater. There is simply no comparison between his reign and that of John, the jovial, jowly father, Dick, the scowling, angst-ridden son, and Prionsias, the silent and holy ghost.

I was late arriving. The ball was as good as over but C. J. H. was supremely courteous and wickedly blunt. Would he comment on the state of the nation? Would he what? 'As they say in Donnycarney, I'll say sweet, bloody nothing.' He misses nothing from his earlier years. 'Not one thing.' So he gave me a lift back to town and he pointed out the northside sights. We talked about the match (off the record); the Blaskets; Paudie Ó Sé taking over the Kerry team; the Beijing women's conference; his wife, Maureen. He does not think many realise her unique experience of politics – the daughter of one Taoiseach, Sean Lemass, the wife of another, both the sister and mother of TDs (the late Noel Lemass and Sean Haughey).

He likes the company of women, likes working with them. They have an intuition that often gives them the edge over men. But he always wondered at how they could do the day job so efficiently as well as rear their families.

So there he was yesterday, as richly bewitching and dead sexy as ever. The most superb example of a man in his prime. Casually dressed in light grey jacket and trousers with an open-necked shirt, he was charming, chivalrous and curious in the sort of way that made you feel you were all that mattered in that brief half-hour.

As for the rest of the men playing politics? Forget it.
You will simply never measure up.

22 September 1995

GIVE THIS GAL THE CROWN

The Panorama *interview that rocked the world. It was the first time a royal was seen on a top current affairs programme and Diana's revenge for some of the punches pulled on her.*

By Georgina, she's done it! And won it. The madwoman has found the key to the attic door. She has escaped. And how. Not screaming hysterically, not hurling curses nor foaming at the mouth, she has come silently down the stairs and confronted Rotter Rochester and his wimpy bimbo.

While RR gasped, reeled, keeled over, while Pale Eye stood rooted to the spot in the house she was beginning to call home, this hitherto silent woman calmly told them – and the listening staff – her side of the story. Throwing the occasional pitying glance and some smelling salts at her husband, she socked it to them. With immense dignity. Without raising her voice, without tears, without self-pity or a hint of indecision, she commanded their undivided attention. Her steely resolve was – as she described bits of her years in the attic – pretty damn devastating. Then she went about her business of reclaiming her 50 per cent of the house, business and booty.

Perfick, as Pop Larkin would say, in his succinct way. Terr-bloody-iffic, I say. Fan-blinking-tastic. In the space of less than sixty minutes last Monday night, Princess Diana did more for the cause of equality for women than all the paid-up written-up feminists of the second dying half of this century. Since little of what they have told us to do is working, they will all just go back to the drawing board again and learn to do it Di's way.

What was her advantage? The secret of her success? Well, hang me, if she did not prove to be the most effective communicator around. She just kept it simple. She told her story straight, candidly and credibly. There were a couple of dimples but not a Dimbleby in sight. And – whether artlessly or artfully – she played up her natural advantages with deadly understatement. She did the doe-eyed bit. Can she help it if she is blessed with large and luminous eyes that can flirt, challenge, or cut you dead with equal effect? The kohl that enhanced them on Monday night was a help but, when the chips were down, was only a tiny part of the equation. Can you blame her for scrunching her mouth up in that wry way that speaks volumes? (It is going to be called the Wry-Di-Nineties-Lips look. No kidding. Millions have already started practising.) Politically that look will prove as potent in the male-ist world of intrigue, gossip, malice or flattery that she has now taken on as Thatcher's famously made-over, softly-softly voice or Boadicea's shield. Just a couple of other survivors in his-herstory.

Another huge plus was the way she spoke. Has anyone ever heard a royal who does not sound as if he or she has deadly difficulty moving the marbles around to let the tongue work? Has anyone ever heard them speak in the first person – they are always 'one-ing' it. 'One feels . . . one does . . . one does not.' Di said 'I'. And she used the language of her generation. 'That ... very nearly did me in' ... 'I was so fed up with being seen as someone who was a basket-case' ... 'I adored him (Hewitt). Yes, I was in love with him.' She was not afraid to talk about love in any context. She had a good, healthy woman's knowledge about postnatal depression and the stigma of silence that often goes with it. As with her bulimia. She spoke frankly and freely about the disease. She did not attempt to hype it up or down. She kept stressing that it was/is a symptom of low self-esteem, of poor self-image. She saw herself as a fat or chubby twenty-year-old with not so much going for her. Nobody disabused her of these ideas. She even blamed herself for sending out the wrong signals to the crowd of buffoons she was living with.

She made people working in the media look deep into their hearts. Particularly women. From here, some can try to dismiss the reporters and photographers who have heavily contributed to her misery as an anonymous Bunch of Them across the water. Do not forget that we pretty well all belong to the same union. We all have to take responsibility. It is up to us to decide what to do with what she rates as 'abusive harassment'.

In a male-led (one woman) panel discussion immediately after on BBC 2's *Newsnight*, they did their best to dismiss and discredit her. At best they just stopped short of calling her a downright liar. Or they let Margaret Jay (using her AIDS-campaigner hat) get in the odd feeble, vaguely supportive line. If she was supposed to be on Di's side, who needs enemies? Other panellists bleated fretfully about the monarchy and all that. Charles's pal Nicholas

Soames had never-ever-ever heard that his mate would not be able to cope with being king. Good heavens. What, what, what? he blustered. And you could tell that this bit of the interview, this fresh assessment of Prince Charles – thrown in at (apparent?) random towards the end – shook Soames. And hence the rest of the establishment.

Not to mention the Family. They are now so well and truly outed you would wonder how they can bear to look at themselves. They can plead ignorance, insanity, inanity, but not innocence of the emotional abuse in their midst. Unless they are all actually more than a bit simple. Di can take them, individually and collectively, to the cleaners. She could take their money, a palace or two and more. They may not have hit her. They may not – literally – have thrown her down the stairs. They just drove her to the point where she hurled herself down any shaft to get away from their mental torture.

Early reaction was shocked and confused. At 5 am on Tuesday the BBC's World Service was getting a mix of reaction. In Sydney, where they saw the interview live, it was unashamedly ecstatic. But – said the man in London rather sternly to the Down Under woman – Australia does not even want the monarchy. Did they not all want to be rid of the royals? The woman had to patiently remind him of Diana's special appeal, her attraction, her charisma. She had to point out that Di is not seen as one of Them. She is, simply, herself. And adored for it.

Somebody in Bonn said reassuring things to London. It was not being taken very seriously, he said. Then he recounted how the whole thing was shown with yards of wedding footage, little-princes' footage and all the rest. So if you heard it as I did: on the one hand nobody in Germany cared a whit, while on the other, they had given it lashings of space and time.

So what is in it for us? For me the issue of most value was that a famous, beautiful woman who would appear to have it all has finally come clean about emotional abuse in the home. And she used one of the best current affairs platforms to do it. On *Panorama* she has talked about the lack of value put on her work by her bosses (albeit family). She has shown the importance she places on family life. She is demanding a proper job. She knows her value and her worth. She wants nothing less than equality. Last week's report from Women's Aid highlighted the high figures of fairly well off middle-class women who suffer from domestic violence. They are the women who never turn up in refuges for battered wives. They are silent statistics. We have all known that they exist. Usually they put up and shut up about their vile lives for a number of reasons, not least because they feel they have too much to lose or are so defeated. They needed a role model. Well, they have got one now.

Princess Diana's life is at a crucial stage. They might try to divorce her off. They could try anything. They will not get that far. One thing is sure: they will not try to patronise her again. If I were them, I'd drop Charles and just give her the top job, crown her queen, when the coronet next comes around.

23 November 1995

131

BLESSED ARE THEY
WITHOUT MEN

The way women continually fall for the old love and romance thing with all its hidden catches never ceases to amaze.

Now we can start the real debate. Not on divorce but on marriage. Why and where did the problems that surround bourgeois coupling get lost in a tide of clichés over the last few months? Those clichés are the old saws that abound in the banalities scattered through the Sweet Valley High school of literature.

My favourite among the chestnuts of this referendum campaign, which had some real classics, was: 'Would you deny them a second chance of happiness?' Happiness? Mother of God. What planet do they think they are on? Did nobody tell them that this is a vale of tears? Literally. That if you manage to get lucky in a average of one out of every twenty years you live, you will be blessed indeed.

Until now, you were probably vaguely aware that people were watching too much television, reading too much *Hello!*, seeing too many movies. Now I am convinced that huge numbers of people of a certain age believe they can have *Sleepless in Seattle* lives. Worse. That they deserve to see strangers across crowded rooms and cleave to them forever. That love and marriage are as indisputably inseparable as horses and carriages. Heaven knows, even horses now have the sense to realise they could lead three lifetimes without ever seeing a carriage, let alone being hooked to one.

More tediously, women and men seem to think that they too can be the guy and the doll in *Mad About You* – an unutterably boring television series seemingly justified by pale plots and the cardboard couple saying they love each other about six thousand times in every half-hour session. The same jargon extends to their friends and relations. Even their in-laws, who should know better, bang on about it as well. 'But I love him/her' is the universal bleat from people all over the place in justification of anything from murder to worse. Do we not all know that such jingles are all very well in Beatles' songs but have precious little to do with real life?

Everlasting re-runs of *Casablanca*, *Dr Zhivago* and suchlike keep the rest of the population in a fuzz of stupor about what life could/should be like. To have loved (Hollywood-style) and lost out in romantically seedy settings is apparently better than to live in the real world where women run their dolls' houses with frantic energy and men lounge around watching sport on the television.

This referendum debate proved that a ridiculously long silly season dominates most people's lives. And it proved that people believe what they see and hear on the silver screen. Next to love, the over- and confused use of the word 'happiness' is probably the greatest example of how Hollywood has come to define our lives. Take the meaning of the H-word in the nearest Collins dictionary. 'Blessed, blest, blissful, blithe, cheerful, content, contented, delighted, ecstatic, jolly, joyful, jubilant, merry . . . ' And so on. I bet a pound to a penny, that if the H-question had been changed to something like: 'Do you not want them to have a second go at bliss/jolliness/jubilation/ecstasy?' many more minds would have been properly focused. Many more people would have seen the whole M-thing for what it is.

Call me what you will –a dried-up old spinster, a kill-joy or a bitter old maid –if it makes you feel better. But it will not change things. I reckon I am lucky to have grown up in a part of the country where I learned young that she who travels fastest and with fun, travels alone. That love and romance have precious little to do with a lifetime of marriage – or even two halves of two marriages – or one-third of three. That marriage, on its own, is a distinctly unglamorous career choice. Much more to do with, if not agony, then unutterable boredom and hard, repetitive work. Precious little ecstasy.

When I was brooding about these things, it was the spinster aunts and middle-aged third cousins who had enchanted lives. They had jobs which gave them smart, polished handbags which they carried every day. Not just for annual outings. They were the ones who slipped you a shilling or a half-crown. Some of them gleamed with the bronze that years spent in dark, exotic countries conferred on them. Others wore prosperous tweed suits and stylish dresses. They even wore earrings. One stands out. She was a priest's housekeeper in America. Not only did she have a fur coat but she always wore a chunky gold bracelet; one charm had a $5 bill wrapped up small to fit a miniature safe. You can't crack that. That was posh. That was living, having it all. Scattered across the wider landscape were women like the district nurse, teachers, the head-waitress in one of the big hotels. Most of them drove their own cars and went on foreign holidays. You heard them described sometimes as 'the ones who never married'. So? When you were young it mattered little. Growing older you sensed the hint of something like tetchy satisfaction in the comment. It still did not matter.

The *realpolitik* of growing up in Kerry was emigration. Many fathers disappeared for significant periods of the year, perhaps to harvest beet in England. I never knew several fathers because they were permanently fixed in Dagenham, Camden Town, Coventry or Luton. Houses were emptied of families and closed up overnight. Most mothers worked hard during the summer season. Some kept people. Others worked in hotels, guesthouses and shops. As we did. It was an unquestioned fact of life.

There were tragedies where the fathers of families died suddenly. They were drowned or electrocuted or were cut down by a quick, fatal disease. It was a time when life insurance was as rare as mortgages. It meant that these dire events dramatically changed the fortunes of a family. Mothers took on two or more jobs. Children left school young. In our family, my father's father had died young, leaving my grandmother to bring up five young boys on a tiny pension. The reality of life was never spelt out. It was never given an 'ism' of any kind. But the stark message that was passed on unsaid, that you picked up unconsciously like the Latin hymns and the litanies that followed the Rosary, was that you got as good an education as possible and then a safe job with a pension. You got a job that would probably be a job for life. If you did get married and gave up, the job should be all the better, to have something to fall back on. There was no sexism and I never remember boys having advantages over girls since only a handful of the lot got as far as university. We were turned into primary school teachers, nurses, civil servants. We got jobs in CIE and the ESB. Those who were forced to leave work on marriage got a fixed sum of money which usually paid the deposit on a house. This transaction was familiar since, even if you did not come from a farming background, you were familiar with the dowry system which continued to exist long after it was spoken about openly. Rural parents were every bit as money-conscious for their children as Jane Austen's mamas and papas. Mr So-and-so's £2,000 a year translated into fields or herds of cattle or the quality of the land. What the wife brought to a marriage was a significant factor – a degree of independence that was never forgotten and gave her an indefinable edge.

I can never understand why matchmaking is so maligned and sent up. It makes infinite sense to have a wide circle of interested adults in on the decision to marry. It makes more sense if the woman has economic independence. Marriage should also carry a civil contract setting out every item of work, care and the contribution of money from both partners; ensuring that equality is set out before the ballyhoo about the guest list and the length of the veil is even begun. Without ring fences like these, I see marriage as a ridiculously poor option for women. It is fine for men – providing them with a valeting, housekeeping and entertainment service. There are exceptions, but for most women marriage is the pits. And that is when it is apparently going OK. Even when you have a husband who will change nappies or do his share of the night shift.

Before the next raft of spring weddings, I advise a good solid debate about the pros and cons, dotting the i's and crossing the t's, making sure there is a written contract and preferably a series of hypnosis treatments to make women forget all the honeyed rubbish they have taken on, osmosis fashion. It is used to entice them into this woeful state. Get wise. Stay a spinster.

30 November 1995

BRUTON POWER,
WIFE POWER

The speech that split the nation was no nine-days' wonder. Its effect lasted into the New Year until the burst of visible violence against women brought a lot of people back to earth.

Thank heaven for Finola Bruton. After my five years of covering women's lives, the furore she caused last week has put the whole thing in context for me. With one fell swoop she has made my stuck-in-a-groove argument about the appallingly selective coverage of women's lives by the media with devastating power.

How? Like a blinding light, she has beamed up the real value of women's lives as they are publicly perceived. The truth is, babes, that the nuts and bolts of your lives or mine do not matter one whit, as far as media coverage goes. Mrs Bruton spoke for ten or fifteen minutes on Friday, but that short interjection in the Clinton visit has managed to get more coverage than any woman-related event – probably since the election of the President. It also obscured any close attention to Hillary Rodham Clinton by giving masses of lineage and space to a little domestic spat.

For years I have been saying that I could get a women-fighting-with-women story into the paper every day. And every day, I could get space for a row about women who are excluded from men's clubs. Those are some of the absolute certainties in the media's perception, not what is important in women's lives. You could follow those up with a few whiny women-as-victim stories. Perhaps a few more about women who are famous by association with powerful/rich/glamorous men. And a few about guilty mammies. As for the rest, forget it. From your personal correspondence to me, from the many women who ring me, from the many others I meet at any number of events, you and I know that the things that matter to you and me are far removed from what goes on in any picture gallery. They are planets away from what goes on in golf and tennis clubs. Would you believe *that* if you were depending on newspapers, radio and television to inform you? You and me, baby, are the soft questions to lighten up the real issues that come up on current affairs programmes. The FB serial makes that clear, once and for all.

As one tiny example; for the nth time, I spent about five hours in Dublin Castle last Monday covering an important EU-related conference. Apart from Mrs Robinson's brief reference to the dangers of phony wars among women – she did not name any name – which was carried in full in this newspaper, the rest of that day's debate was compressed into a few paragraphs. Just for the hell of it let me tell you some of the names and the issues raised at that conference. There were two women ministers, Niamh Bhreathnach and Nora Owen. There was Mary O'Rourke, deputy leader of Fianna Fáil. There was Mo Mowlam, British Opposition spokeswoman on Northern Ireland. The British Ambassador was observing some of the proceedings. The other women who spoke read like a

Who's Who of women doing important jobs. They were a fair sample of the numbers of women achievers in this country. There was Frances Gardiner, politics lecturer, who organised the seminar; Paulyn Marrinan-Quinn, insurance ombudsman; Margaret Hennessey, a former Irish Ambassador; TDs Liz O'Donnell and Frances Fitzgerald; Gemma Hussey, former Minister; Ruth Barrington from the Department of Health; Miriam Hederman-O'Brien, who is fairly impossible to categorise since she has been involved in so many things; Hilary Henry, managing director of Lakeshore Foods, and in Bord Bia and who is also on a county enterprise board; Darina Allen, cookery supremo; Joan McGinley, the Joan of Arc of campaigners in marine and fishing; Gertie Shields of Mothers Against Drunken Driving; Olive Braiden, director of the Dublin Rape Crisis Centre; Kathleen Maher, former chairwoman of the National Campaign for the Homeless, and the amazing eighty-six-year-old Eleanor MacDonald, from Women in Management UK.

Get it? That was just one conference in one day in Dublin. And the names are just some of the speakers. They don't include the one hundred and fifty plus audience of women, many of whom are well known in various fields. As at the majority of these seminars, I was the only reporter.

Who cares? Nobody with any power in the media obviously. They just take out the video of *The Politician's Wife* to find out about women and politics. Equally interesting is the story I got on the FB affair. Unfortunately it has too much commonsense to be considered, and no slagging matches. It simply, babes, is not sexy enough.

Because I am infinitely weary at the never-mind-the-substance approach to coverage of women's lives I talked to a number of people at the weekend –several of them in Fine Gael who, understandably, did not want to be named. Briefly, the politicians I spoke to were asking serious questions that demand serious answers. Like, how much of that speech was part of the wider Fine Gael political agenda? When can the spouse of a politician speak on a serious topic and if s/he is a government spouse, how much of what they say is part of government policy? Is there a special unknown spouse-agenda for the Taoiseach's wife?

One senior Fine Gael deputy said: 'The most important thing to be established is the status of the speech. Who sanctioned it? It is clear we need a debate on the political position of the wife of the Taoiseach to set the record straight for the future.' Two Fine Gael sources said it was well known within the party that several dominant landowners and businessmen who backed the party were less than enchanted with John Bruton for (as things stand) getting the country to vote for divorce. 'Was this speech an attempt to build bridges with the core supporters of Fine Gael? Would Finola Bruton have made this speech a week before the referendum?' one asked. Another asked: if Mrs Bruton seriously believed that all women were better off in the home, how much of this influenced FG thinking on women as politicians? In the 1980s FG led the way in actively recruiting and promoting women. What is the end-of-century agenda of the party?

More spoke about the secrecy that surrounded the whole thing. The National Women's Council (funded by the government) who were hosting the do in the gallery with the US Embassy, were asked to include Mrs Bruton 'at a late date'. When they asked to see her speech they were told that she would be talking about the achievements of women. Oh yeah.

Most people who know Finola Bruton like her. I interviewed her some years ago and enjoyed it so much I wanted to sit all day around the roaring fire talking about everything. She is good company, adores politics and is an obvious advantage to her husband as well as her children. She held the same views then as now. She has since given much the same speech at a few public functions. They were not reported. I would take most things she has said seriously. Instead, the message on this occasion got lost in the fog of reaction and counter-reaction. All that fuss will continue to ripple along predictably. And it will fade, like any nine-days' wonder. It is up to you, babes. Do you want to be treated like real people? Or is it good enough to be considered a batch of Barbies?

7 December 1995

MURDER, MAIMING AND MAYHEM

Marilyn Rynn's murder near her home on the night of her office Christmas party hit the public consciousness with particular ferocity. She was a woman many could identify with, a civil servant, independent and well liked. Her death started the New Year of 1996 with a new high in crimes against women and a new low in our so-called traditional values. A man was subsequently charged with her murder.

Is this it? Is this what you call living? Look around. Read the headlines. Not even two weeks into 1996, ask yourself if this is the Ireland you want to live in for the rest of the year? For the rest of your life? In the name of all that is sacred, what kind of psychotic little statelet is this? Who the hell is supposed to be in charge?

For the rest of 1996, for the rest of the waning century, do you too want to live in fear of taking a short-cut home? Do you want your life destroyed by rape, murder and assault? Do you want your elderly mothers and fathers living around the country beaten up and viciously attacked in their homes? Do you want contract killers riding around on motor bikes at high speed to their next hit? Do you want to go home and – like one colleague last week – find your house turned upside down with your few precious possessions, like your mother's wedding ring, taken by louts who will never be caught. Even if they are, it will make little difference to their careers. But their assault on your mind or body will leave you demented for months and maybe for life.

Do you want to continue living in a country where the compromises women make in order to survive now amount to us living under siege, confined to virtual house arrest? We sneak out in daylight to go to work. We sit in cars with the doors locked but still feeling unsafe if we are caught in traffic or even held up by the lights. We know, only too well, that windows can be smashed, that we'll be lucky if just our bags are taken. If that is all that happens, we know we will try to reassure ourselves with learned and pitiful little jingles like: 'Sure, it could have been worse'. Or 'It was only money'. Or 'I'll just have to be more careful'. Or 'It happens in London, Paris and New York, we can't expect to escape in Dublin/ Cork/Galway/Limerick/Tralee or Connemara'.

Are we now so fooled and frightened into such conditioned and despairing responses that we are struck dumb this week at the murder of Marilyn Rynn? Are we so intimidated that we sit silently, under a shroud of hopelessness, waiting for the next attack? Have we begun to believe the unspoken but still deeply felt view that, in some way – regardless of the horror of the crime – we have asked for it? Are we shivering under the cloud of pervasive guilt simply for being women? Do we believe that for just having been created women we must put up with a regime of crime and punishment that nearly always leaves some of the mud of the sins of men sticking to us? Have we accepted the largely unspoken notions that the price for being independent women means we have to live out our lives under more and more limiting curfews? And if we depart one iota from the set rules, we can be prepared to expect the worst?

No. We do not. No. We cannot. No. We will not. We have to shout 'Stop'. We (not so simple) have to turn the whole question round and look at the facts. What is vividly clear is that this country is critically out of control. It is politically, morally and spiritually leaderless and rudderless. The only politics practised is that which belongs to the world of balancing the accounts, of being able to say we have the lowest inflation in recent history, of piling up points in bringing the wars of other countries to an end, of being seen on the TV shaking hands with the Mr Xs, Mr Ys or Mr Zees on the international circuit. The bottom line is about holding seats, about the kudos can be stacked up in the short time between elections. The only morality is a quagmire of meaningless rubbish put out by the old men desperate to hold on to the power they lost when they still lived comfortably in a world of impenetrable palaces.

A spiritual bankruptcy exists in the vacuum created by years of lack of real contact between churchmen and us, and their cosmic ignorance and indifference about our lives. Since they have failed so abysmally in tackling their own problems, pretending that if they do not speak about them they will go away, they have lost most of us and left the rest floundering. So we carry on with our own notions of spirituality and hope for the best. And the best of them go to the Third World.

It is not enough. It is both pitiable and outrageous. Do

they not yet know that women's lives are not solely defined by issues like abortion and divorce? Why do they persist only in sermonising and sending out scripts at times when these two chestnuts are on the table again? For how much longer will they persist in regretting that women have learned how to speak and, more importantly, to question and talk back? For how long will they dismiss the prospect of women getting their jobs? Why, in this most awful and tragic of weeks, with the discovery of Marilyn Rynn's body as the first brutal harbinger of what will happen to more women in 1996, is there not any public word from any bishop or archbishop? What do they feel? What do they think? What are they doing? Not just about women but about the men who do such desperate deeds?

And let's not just question the way men appointed to arbitrate on justice, good and evil do their work. Today Des Hanafin will be in the High Court in his attempt to get the divorce referendum nullified. While he is taking the case as a private citizen, he is also a leading 'pro-life' campaigner. Why is there a deathly silence from him, William Binchy et al about the murder of a forty-one-year-old woman on her way home from a night out? How can they expect to be taken seriously about the lives of foetuses if the unborn is all they ever speak out about?

Neither can Nora Bennis nor the National Women's Council nor the small but significant number of women prominent in politics and other areas be let off the hook. Why are their fax machines strangely quiet this week? One can understand the weariness of many of them. Crimes like this and other horrendous deeds against women have happened before. They have all done their share of protesting, of marching and of writing about them. But do they not realise that it is the their actions on such issues or those of women who went before them that have got them into the jobs they now enjoy?

Why is there no clamour for the Dáil to be recalled? Is everybody content to sit around waiting for the Budget which, you can bet, will have precious little money for dealing with things like crimes against women or investigation of the reasons why men are committing them? Not just the perceived reasons – the real ones, which emerge only from careful and costly research. God knows, we all need a cut in our taxes but we also urgently need a debate on whether paying less tax is preferable to not being able to walk the streets with safety. Do we need more prisons? What we definitely want is more gardaí on the beat.

Last Friday, my elderly mother answered a knock on the door around lunchtime. It was a fine, bright Kerry day. I was inside, picking at the unending leftovers, and nearly choked when she told a man – a stranger – who said he was selling potatoes that she would not possibly get through a stone-weight bagful. 'I live on my own. I only use a small amount,' she said. It is a measure of my fear of living in this little island, as we head into another year, that I could only see horror headlines as a result of such a simple and common rural interchange.

Am I over-reacting? As Gay Byrne says, talk to me. And if Finola Bruton's husband is saying nothing, what does she think?

11 January 1996

MY FATHER, THE SERGEANT

This reflective piece probably grew out of the awful things now commonplace in Irish life. It must have said things to a huge number of people since I got more response to this than to anything previously written. Warmly favourable letters and calls came from all over the country from people who had grown up in similar surroundings – partly thanks to Gay Byrne, who read some of the piece on his radio programme and reached listeners who are not normally Irish Times *readers.*

The paraphernalia of coming from a garda household littered my childhood and continues to pervade the various ways I view life and people. The barracks (where we lived in 'the quarters') was a powerhouse of activity. We were at the centre of things. Even in winter when it appeared there was nothing much happening, the County Kerry barracks hummed along, fuelled by an energy of its own and the things it dealt with.

Even when the summer tourists had gone, the schools had reopened, the emigrants had returned to Harlesden, Camden Town or New York, and the extra guards drafted in for the season were scattered, there was a new, but no less exacting, routine for my father and three or four guards who were there all year round.

The barracks in Ballybunion is in a commanding position, taking up one side of the square. From its windows you can look down the Main Street, up Church Road and see all the incoming traffic from Tralee, Listowel or Limerick. It is a big rambling house with a long landing upstairs and wide window-seats everywhere. You could sit reading, hidden behind the curtains. We had no inside bathroom for a couple of years. Then a small bedroom was turned into one, leaving me with an abiding yearning for bathrooms that are real rooms. In the 1950s, 1960s and into the 1970s, the barracks was a caravanserai at the centre of things. The guards did the census and much else of an official nature. People came to get passports, references, requests to find missing relatives in England, to look for advice if they were thinking of taking a civil case to court – often over land – or to get a young man to marry the girl he had got into trouble.

There was little or no welfare and I remember my father sending women, widowed or deserted, or men with problems to Dan Spring, our local Labour TD. My parents never discussed politics but it was taken as read that it was Dan Spring who got things done.

You could set your watch by my father. He went out our back door, crossed the yard and went in the back door of the barracks at 9.20 am precisely every weekday except Mondays. On Mondays, they had a special inspection and drill in the day-room at 9 am sharp. His uniform, which was always spick-and-span, got a special damp-ironing that day. He polished his shoes until you could see yourself in them. He Silvo-ed his buttons, using a special gadget that fitted around the buttons, so that the liquid did not get on the material. My mother would brush down the back of his jacket. His hat was put on with a little more care on Mondays and court days.

At one minute to 1 pm he recrossed the yard and came back into the kitchen for dinner. Afterwards, he sat in the enormous armchair near the range and read the paper. Sometimes he closed his eyes and appeared to doze. After the *Topical Talk* on the radio, he would ruffle his paper again. He was always gone by ten to two. At twenty to four, he came back again for a cup of tea and a couple of plain biscuits. Then he donned a gaberdine coat in winter, or a light tweed sports jacket in summer, called the dog and often one of us, and set off down the Main Street. At five to four exactly he dropped a bundle of official brown envelopes with a harp on them into the letterbox outside the post-office – the post was collected at 4 pm. There was never a day when he did not have a decent handful of letters to send off.

In summer, we went to the strand for a swim. In winter (after the Listowel Races until Easter or Whit) we (or he on his own) would go for a long, brisk walk back the Long Strand, or up and down the now-eroded path on the sandhills that skirted the golf course. Sometimes he would go all the way to the Cashen River, and come back by the road, calling in at the graveyard to inspect new graves – about six or seven miles in all. He like walking but he and the guards also often cycled out the country. They were sometimes on official business but nonetheless stopped to talk to farmers working in fields or in their haggards. There were regular houses where they would have a cup of tea or a drink of water.

A few times a year we would go on a really long walk to the Hill and down the other side. In that flat part of north Kerry, the Hill is simplistically named but it has a heroic past. Its real name is Cnoc an Áir (massacre), and it is where Fionn and the Fianna are supposed to have fought a bloody battle with invaders. You went up past Doon Church, to Rahavannig and Derra – the dividing line between us and Ballylongford. Lahasreagh, Ballynoneen and down by Moohane and Ahafona and back up the village by East End. On this walk, the townlands merged into one another. My father knew them all. He knew where each one started and finished. He knew who was in every house, who had died there, who had emigrated and who had troubles. He might tell you things, but not much. He was compulsively, obsessively secretive – or perhaps it was just discretion. Sometimes he would spell things backwards for my mother and we would try to guess a word here and there. Sometimes they would talk in Irish. We would try to keep up. But there was an implicit, unspoken rule that we never repeated anything outside the house. Usually we had little interest.

This undefined discretion permeated to the wives of the guards. They had a special relationship. While they were part of the general life of the town – the ICA, cleaning the brasses in the church or whatever, they also had a particular friendship with each other. Often it was only the jobs of their spouses they had in common but that close, almost familial thing existed between, like a mantle of responsibility. This clannish rapport between garda families was a universal thing. When someone got promoted or someone else's child did particularly well in any field, it was almost as good as if it had been one of us. We picked things up by chance and stored them away. For example, there was no bank in Ballybunion for much of my childhood. A lending agency in Cork used to ring my father to find out about people's creditworthiness. If he took the call on the phone extension in our hall, we would overhear the conversation by staying very quiet on the landing upstairs or opening the door of the back kitchen a fraction. 'Yes, he's fine,' he would say. 'A good farm of land there. They're an industrious family.' Or he would urge caution. 'Well, I wouldn't give him that much. Maybe half. They say she is bringing a good dowry with her, but nothing definite is settled yet.'

Sometimes, late at night, women would ring, their voices shrill with bitterness and anger. They wouldn't give their names but demanded that such-and-such a pub or hotel be raided. Usually it was because their husbands were holed up, drinking after hours, unwilling to go home.

My father was famous for his strictness, his authority and his sense of duty. He came from that generation of sergeants and guards who were never off duty. If the barracks was closed, people just came round to our door. The phone was always turned over. He never took days off and had only minimal holidays to visit relations. The shelves in the pantry off the kitchen were laden with bottles of whiskey, brandy and sherry which the publicans and hoteliers delivered faithfully every Christmas Eve. I used to wonder why they bothered since he continued to raid them all with assiduous regularity. Brendan Kennelly says he and his pals always had to give duty dances to the sergeant's daughters, feeling it might lessen the penalty if they were caught without a light on their bikes going home.

My father used quaint language when talking about some 'clients' as he described them in a withering tone. He would call some of them 'blackguards' or 'real blackguards'. A rogue or a rascal was a lesser evil.

We often went to sleep to the howls and rich, roaring language of the drunks in the lock-up, which faced on to the back yard. They would bang the door, curse and swear until they passed out, exhausted, in the tiny cell.

My father was a tall, tidy, meticulous man with neat, distinctive writing. His own father had been in the RIC and had died young, leaving my grandmother with five young boys to rear on a small pension. My father's pride in the Garda Síochána or 'the force' as he usually referred to it, was cosmic. There was no other body of men like it, no better members, no higher standards. He died the year after he retired in 1975 – twenty-one years ago tomorrow.

1 February 1996

TO HELL WITH
FLORENCE NIGHTINGALE

*For the first time we see nurses behave in the way they
are forced to if they are ever going to get real money
rather than platitudes.*

Last Friday on RTE Radio One's *Morning Ireland*, Michael
Noonan pressed the 'God bless our Nurses' button and
jump-started the old, familiar worn-out tune. Irish nurses
are . . . are known all over the world . . . are the best
qualified . . . the most compassionate. And other such
sentiments. This spiel is done in low, reverential tones.
Any minute you expected a Gregorian chant to moan softly
in the background.

But last Friday was different. Áine Lawlor's voice
brought the record to a sharp stop. She reminded the
Minister for Health of the here and now. These nurses, she
said briskly, were a very angry lot of workers. What was he
going to do about them? Then you got the more-in-sorrow-
than-in-anger bit. Did he not put £10 million on the table?
And then? Well, Áine, didn't he huff and puff at the Cabinet
table? Then didn't he tack on another £10 million? And
sure, there's no money left. At all. At all. He sighed.

Minister Noonan will do a lot more than sighing before
this rout of himself and his department is over. For the
first time, I can hear the swell of despair among nurses
turned into a steely anger. For the first time, I sense a calm

154

and united resolution of purpose. For the first time, there is a mature assessment among nurses of their notoriously under-valued work. There is an awakening that has been long in coming but once it is here, there is no going back. In fact, for most nurses, it hardly matters who the Minister for Health is at the moment. It is the anonymous civil servants in Health and Finance who have been outed as the real decision-makers. Once again, they are showing their incredible ignorance and foolhardy arrogance in their niggardly dealing with the issue of nurses' pay and conditions. Once more, with little feeling, they are taking the usual put-up-or-shut-up line. They know that, regardless of what they do, their own substantial salaries will continue to plop through the letterboxes at the end of every month. They know that when their working lives of solid backsides on comfortable chairs are over, satisfyingly index-linked pensions will continue to cushion them from reality.

But Minister Noonan should worry. He is the one who will be facing the nurses, their families and patients – who are doomed to further unnecessary suffering – at the next election. In twelve months or less, he will be facing a helluva lot of Nos if he continues to listen to the chorus of 'yes Minister' people who run his life. They have already done enough damage by ridiculously trying to trap the lives and work of nurses in a league of bureaucratic piffle. One of the many signs that this dispute is totally different to any in the past showed up this week in *The Irish Times* Letters to the Editor. It was from Maeve Dwyer and Peta Taaffe. It did not say they are matrons of the National Maternity Hospital, Holles Street and St James's Hospital, respectively.

Hospital matrons do not lightly write to newspapers in the middle of a dispute. Neither do they usually say in public what Ms Dwyer and Ms Taaffe said in their letter.

It said, in part: 'If these negotiations are allowed to drag on until nurses have to consider strike action, we in Ireland stand to lose far more than we could possibly gain by delaying or limiting a pay increase. We have a compassionate, caring and well-motivated work force which, if driven to such industrial action, we are likely to lose forever. There is an urgent need to correct pay anomalies which have arisen over several years. The strength of feeling among nurses was recently demons-trated when over two thousand attended a meeting in Dublin. If Irish society places any value on the service provided by nurses this is the time to demonstrate it.'

The days of silent servility are long over. The days when nurses muttered among themselves but kept up the bright face of professionalism for the public are gone. For too long, many of them believed the clap-trap about being angels of mercy, saints or professionals who did not grumble about sordid things like money. When I did midwifery at the Rotunda Hospital, twenty-odd years ago, there was nothing more awful than when you had to accompany a woman and her husband to their car and accept a box of chocolates when you handed over Gráinne or Oisín. It was embarrassing for nurses and patients. The mother knew you were paid buttons, but in some way, she was trying to show her appreciation for the bit of attention she had got. It was often middle-of-the-night sort of attention – the shoulder to blubber on, the encouragement to continue breast-feeding or the assurance to tell her to relax, buy bags of formula and the bonding would be just as good – which made the difference in the way patients evaluated their experience in hospitals.

It was still more embarrassing for patients who did not have anything to give a nurse for whom they had developed a special fondness: when they felt their time in hospital had been immeasurably improved by one nurse or the staff of one ward. They did not feel they owed anything special to doctors, physiotherapists, radiographers, lab technicians or porters. They certainly did not feel they owed much to the god-almighty who came and went amid great pomp and ceremony, muttered things to his retinue and left the nurse to translate the outcome of his deliberations. What the officials at the Departments of Health and Finance do not realise is that today's nurses are no longer prepared to put up either with real roses or rosy platitudes. Clichés are kaput. Most qualified nurses and a significant number of student nurses are working mothers. They pay childminders. Cars are a necessity. Mortgages are essential. Because there was no work for many of them when they qualified, by now they have been abroad and seen the lifestyles of their colleagues in other countries. Conditions and pay at home sag painfully by comparison.

In the last ten years I have seen the nursing profession lose many potentially terrific workers and shapers of the future because of the slapdash quality of nurses' education. Particularly so after the deadly cutbacks in 1987, when young nurses were turned loose on wards with little preparation. They were confronted with the lethal combination of numbingly tiring, challenging work and a hierarchical system that subdued them into silence. They saw their friends, with much the same points, going to university and becoming 'ologists' of one kind or another. The friends' lives seemed free and full in comparison with theirs. There were not enough trained staff to show them that things would get better; or to tell them that the job satisfaction in nursing is among the highest in any profession. The best often left.

What officials in government departments have obviously not yet learned is that young women (and a growing number of men) who have chosen nursing as a career see it as a job for life. They want to be well educated for a job which will be rewarding financially as well as in other ways, as they grow older. They do not want bad backs for life because they are forced to lift patients on their own. They will not put up with a job that keeps them in a state of genteel penury most of their lives.

In the absence of a couldn't-care-less attitude from the Department of Health for many years, the debate about their future has been developed by nurses, their organisations and unions – which have finally seen the worth of strength of unity and numbers – and the far-seeing members of the Irish Matrons' Association. Over the years of apparent vacuum, an energised confidence has been gradually replacing the apathy of nurses. The ballot papers have gone out – with recommendations that nurses turn down the ridiculous proposals from Minister Noonan. The result will be known on or before the twenty-ninth of this month.

It needs to be – and I believe will be – resounding. Who believes tall stories about the money not being there? Proinsias De Rossa could get £195 million last year to compensate women who were due social welfare arrears. The most important issue in the nurses' dispute is a serious arrears in attitude to nurses in the Department of Health, from the top down.

8 February 1996